"Bring the Classics to Life"

THE HOUND OF THE BASKERVILLES

Level 5

Series Designer
Philip J. Solimene

Editor
Deborah Tiersch-Allen

EDCON
Long Island, N.Y.

Story Adaptor

Geraldine Lettieri

Author

Sir Arthur Conan Doyle

Copyright © 1992
A/V Concepts Corp.
Long Island, New York

Printed IN U.S.A.
ISBN 0-931334-67-5

CONTENTS

Words Used 4, 5

WORDS USED

Story 11	Story 12	Story 13	Story 14	Story 15

KEY WORDS

Story 11	Story 12	Story 13	Story 14	Story 15
admiral	advantage	exhausted	attract	chilly
bitter	afterward	knob	connect	froze
civilized	humor	maple	convince	knelt
construction	lack	Mister	exhaust	shudder
peril	librarian	sofa	expedition	stubborn
transportation	tickle	widow	interval	toboggan

NECESSARY WORDS

Story 11	Story 12	Story 13	Story 14	Story 15
examine		heir	leads	mansion
manuscript		investigation	pounds	prehistoric
moor		supernatural	telegram	quicksand

WORDS USED

Story 16	Story 17	Story 18	Story 19	Story 20
KEY WORDS				
fiord	abandon	atmosphere	crystal	conscious
funeral	frantic	entrance	delicate	dread
horizon	ignore	inspect	detail	fling
ivory	panic	relax	oxygen	flip
parka	poisonous	resolution	souvenir	pressure
relative	witness	suggestion	tourist	rudder
NECESSARY WORDS				
convict	financial	appointment	muzzle	
developments		photographs	paralyzed	
extraordinary		portrait		
		warrant		

Sherlock Holmes

PREPARATION

Key Words

admiral	(ad′ mər əl)	a naval officer of the highest rank *The officer that the sailors saluted is the admiral.*
bitter	(bit′ ər)	sharp; painful; severe *We stayed home from school because of the bitter cold.*
civilized	(siv′ ə līzd)	advanced in social customs, art, and science; refined *In civilized countries, most people know how to read and write.*
construction	(kən struk′ shən)	the act of building something *Grandfather spent twenty years in the construction of his model ships.*
peril	(per′ əl)	danger *When the truck rolled over, the driver was in great peril.*
transportation	(trans′ pər tā shən)	ways of carrying people and things *Buses and trucks are familiar forms of transportation.*

Sherlock Holmes

Necessary Words

examine (eg zam′ ən) look at closely, carefully inspect
The child wanted to <u>examine</u> each piece of the puzzle before putting them <u>together</u>.

manuscript (man′ yə skript) book or paper written by hand or with a typewriter
The neatly typed <u>manuscript</u> was the result of years of study and experience.

moor (mur) open wasteland; heather may grow on it
Low, evergreen shrubs with small pink or purple flowers covered the entire <u>moor</u> like grass in an open field.

People

Sherlock Holmes is a famous English detective.

Dr. Watson is Sherlock Holmes' friend and assistant.

Dr. Mortimer is a man who is seeking Sherlock Holmes' help.

Places

London is the capital city of the United Kingdom of Great Britain and Northern Ireland, in S.E. England on the Thames.

Sherlock Holmes

Dr. Mortimer read the legend of the Hound of the Baskervilles to Sherlock Holmes and Dr. Watson.

Preview: 1. Read the name of the story.
                  2. Look at the picture.
                  3. Read the sentence under the picture.
                  4. Read the first 3 paragraphs of the story.
                  5. Then answer the following question.

You learned from your preview that
____ a.   the story is told by Sherlock Holmes.
____ b.   Sherlock Holmes lost his walking stick.
____ c.   the story is told by someone named Watson.
____ d.   Sherlock Holmes and Watson are enemies.

Turn to the Comprehension Check on page 10 for the right answer.

Now read the story.

Read to find out what new adventure awaits Sherlock Holmes.

Sherlock Holmes

Mr. Sherlock Holmes, the great detective, was seated at the table in his apartment on Baker Street in London. He was usually very late to breakfast in the morning. Today was not any different.

I was standing by the fireplace on this bitter cold morning holding a fine wooden walking stick. Our visitor had left it behind the night before. We had missed him and had no idea what it was he wanted.

"Well Watson, now that you have examined the stick, what do you think of the man who left it?"

"The initials, *M.R.C.S.* suggest that James Mortimer is a doctor. He is not a town doctor, however, for this stick is worn, used by a man whose foremost means of transportation are his feet. Dr. Mortimer is a country doctor. I suspect the *C.C.H.* has something to do with a hunt. Dr. Mortimer might have given care to a hunter."

Although Holmes was impressed with my views, he set about the construction of Dr. Mortimer.

"My dear man, you have helped me find truth with your errors!" he said. "For instance, Dr. Mortimer was given the walking stick from a hospital rather than from a hunt; *C.C.H.* represents Charing Cross Hospital. The man practiced in town first, then went into practice in the country. Also, Dr. Mortimer has a dog. Observe the teeth marks on the stick."

As Holmes was solving the mystery of the walking stick, he noticed a dog outside on the doorstep.

"Dr. Mortimer will soon be with us, Watson."

At that moment, a reply to a knock at the door brought us face-to-face with James Mortimer. Mortimer was joyful, most civilized, when he saw the walking stick. He believed that he might have left it at the Shipping Office the day before.

More of Mortimer's character became clear as he was questioned about his past. He was not a doctor, but a man interested in science. Further discovery showed that Mortimer left the hospital because he had married. Indeed, the walking stick was a gift to him by two friends at the Charing Cross Hospital.

"I have come to you, Mr. Holmes, because you absorb details, have a mind keen for curiosity, and possess a practical attention for facts. I have an old manuscript for you to examine."

Mortimer took the manuscript from his coat. The writer of the manuscript began his tale with hope for pardon in the Baskerville family; as Mortimer read on, the legend began to unfold.

"Hugo Baskerville, the first of the family, was not civilized. His taste for cruel actions was known to many people. This Hugo came to love a young woman who was the daughter of a yeoman. Her family held lands near the Baskervilles, but were not as rich as an admiral's family might be. Since the position of the woman's father was not of an admiral, Hugo believed he could carry off the young woman when her father and brothers were not at home. She was placed in an upstairs chamber in Baskerville Hall, but escaped when the time was right.

"Hugo discovered the woman had run away. Angry and bitter at her action, he cried out that he would give his body and soul to the Powers of Evil if he could capture the young woman. His friends were drunk and angry and told him to release the hounds upon her. Each hound was shown the maiden's scarf and given her scent for the hunt.

"Hugo mounted his mare for transportation and let loose the hounds on the darkness of the moor. Hugo's friends suddenly came to their senses and realized that the woman was in great peril. They, too, mounted their horses and started across the moor.

"A shepherd, half-crazy, gave a description of the unhappy woman and the hounds on her trail. 'But I saw more than that!' the shepherd stated in a startling speech. 'Hugo Baskerville passed by on his black mare. Behind him ran a hound - running as if the devil was after him! Heaven forbid a hound like that should ever run after me!'

"Later, Hugo's friends saw a black mare approach them. Some of the men rode towards a clearing with the aid of the bright moon. The scene raised the hair upon their heads. In the center of the clearing lay the woman, fallen dead of fear in heart, weary worn in body. Hugo Baskerville lay dead near her. The men shuddered when they saw the horrible thing as it plucked at Hugo's throat. It was a great, black beast shaped like a hound, but much larger than any man had ever seen. The beast tore out Hugo's throat as if it had a right to punish him. With blazing eyes and dripping jaws, it turned to attack the three men who watched in disgust. They rode away to save their lives, screaming across the moor.

"To this day, the family remains unhappy in deaths which have been sudden, bloody, and filled with mystery. They pray to God for release, not to be punished for a past cruel deed. Watch then with care when a Baskerville crosses the moor in those dark hours when the Powers of Evil are stirring."

The manuscript was signed by Hugo Baskerville, a descendant of the evil Hugo, to his sons, Rodger and John.

Mortimer finished reading. "Do you not find it interesting?" he asked.

"To a collector of fairy tales," said Holmes, yawning.

Sherlock Holmes

COMPREHENSION CHECK

Choose the best answer.

1. Watson thought that Mortimer traveled mostly on foot because
   ___ a. Mortimer's shoes were worn out.
   ___ b. Mortimer's walking stick was worn.
   ___ c. Mortimer's walking stick had teeth marks on it.
   ___ d. Mortimer lived in the city.

2. Holmes knew that Mortimer would arrive soon because
   ___ a. he heard footsteps.
   ___ b. they had set a time to meet.
   ___ c. he saw a dog outside.
   ___ d. he saw Mortimer coming.

3. Mortimer came to see Sherlock Holmes to
   ___ a. buy a walking stick from him.
   ___ b. give him a walking stick for a gift.
   ___ c. treat him for an illness.
   ___ d. show him an old manuscript.

4. The writer of the tale described Hugo Baskerville as
   ___ a. cruel.
   ___ b. friendly.
   ___ c. having a keen mind.
   ___ d. being interested in science.

5. First, Hugo Baskerville carried off the young woman. Then, she escaped. Next,
   ___ a. Hugo placed her in an upstairs chamber.
   ___ b. Hugo released the hounds.
   ___ c. the woman was killed.
   ___ d. Hugo was killed.

6. In the clearing, Hugo Baskerville's friends saw
   ___ a. a half-crazy shepherd.
   ___ b. Sherlock Holmes.
   ___ c. a huge black dog.
   ___ d. a woman running in fear.

7. The writer of the manuscript believes that the Baskervilles
   ___ a. continue to be punished for Hugo's cruel deed.
   ___ b. are not as rich as their neighbors.
   ___ c. are a very happy family.
   ___ d. have nothing to worry about.

8. Sherlock Holmes yawned and called the manuscript a "fairy tale" because
   ___ a. it was past his bedtime.
   ___ b. he thought the story was true.
   ___ c. he thought the story was made up.
   ___ d. he liked fairy tales.

9. Another name for this story could be
   ___ a. "An Amusing Tale."
   ___ b. "A Tale of Terror."
   ___ c. "Dr. Mortimer's Stick."
   ___ d. "A Surprise for Sherlock Holmes."

10. This story is mainly about
    ___ a. the history of the Baskervilles.
    ___ b. the curiosity of Sherlock Holmes.
    ___ c. an unhappy young woman.
    ___ d. Watson's clever guesses.

Check your answers with the key on page 67.

Sherlock Holmes

VOCABULARY CHECK

admiral	bitter	civilized	construction	peril	transportation

I. Sentences to Finish

Fill in the blank in each sentence with the correct key word from the box above.

1. The ship was in _____ because of the approaching hurricane.

2. Jet planes are an important means of _____ .

3. Ben spent many hours on the _____ of his model racing car.

4. When _____ winds blow, we want to stay indoors.

5. The explorers were surprised to find that the country was _____ .

6. The _____ ordered the fleet to sail.

II. Making Sense of Sentences

Do the statements below make sense? Place an X next to the correct answer.

1. The first step in the <u>construction</u> of a building is to knock out all the windows. _____ True_____ False

2. If you were in <u>peril</u>, you would probably be frightened. _____ True_____ False

3. An <u>admiral</u> probably knows a great deal about ships. _____ True_____ False

4. The United States today is a <u>civilized</u> nation. _____ True_____ False

5. The most delicious foods are those that have a <u>bitter</u> taste. _____ True_____ False

6. Radio and television are used for <u>transportation</u>. _____ True_____ False

Check your answers with the key on page 69.

The Death of Sir Charles Baskerville

PREPARATION

Key Words

advantage	(ad van′ tij)	something that is in one's favor *Joyce found living near a lake an advantage in learning to swim.*
afterward	(af′ tər wərd)	at a later time *Mark didn't go with us to the movie; afterward, he was sorry he missed it.*
humor	(hyü′ mər)	that which makes people laugh *Sally didn't see any humor in the joke Jim played on her.*
lack	(lak)	to want or need; be without; have none *I would like to play baseball, but I lack a catcher's glove.*
librarian	(lī brer′ ē ən)	a person who takes care of a library *Mr. Winter, the librarian, always helps me find interesting books to read.*
tickle	(tik′ əl)	to touch another person in a way that will cause laughter *You can make Sam laugh if you tickle him.*

The Death of Sir Charles Baskerville

People

Sir Charles Baskerville   was a kind, wealthy man and the master of Baskerville Hall.

Barrymore   is the butler at Baskerville Hall.

Places

Baskerville Hall   is the large home that has been occupied by the Baskerville family for many years.

The Death of Sir Charles Baskerville

Dr. Mortimer told Sherlock Holmes all the facts he had gathered on the night of Sir Charles' death.

Preview:
1. Read the name of the story.
2. Look at the picture.
3. Read the sentence under the picture.
4. Read the first two paragraphs of the story.
5. Then answer the following question.

You learned from your preview that
___ a. Sir Charles Baskerville was still living.
___ b. Sir Charles Baskerville had never been ill.
___ c. Sir Charles Baskerville was a poor but honest man.
___ d. Sir Charles Baskerville was a kind and generous man.

Turn to the Comprehension Check on page 16 for the right answer.

Now read the story.

Read to find out why the death of Sir Charles Baskerville brings fear to Doctor Mortimer.

The Death of Sir Charles Baskerville

Dr. Mortimer read aloud a newspaper which gave the facts about the death of Sir Charles Baskerville. Holmes and I listened carefully.

"Neighbors had found Sir Charles generous. He did not lack good character or good humor. The Baskerville countryside was quiet enough for a librarian. Sir Charles had the advantage of a very large sum of money earned in South Africa. Because he did not lack kindness, the entire countryside benefited from his good fortune. No foul play was suspect in his death. Since his wife's death, Sir Charles had lived a quiet life. His indoor servants were Barrymore the butler and his housekeeper wife. For some time, Sir Charles had attacks of breathlessness and less good humor. He had been happy and in good health before his wife's death, but afterward, Dr. Mortimer declared that Sir Charles became ill.

"Each evening he would eat dinner; afterward, he would take a walk down to the Yew Alley. But on the night of June 4th, when he went for his walk, he never returned. At midnight, Barrymore was worried because Sir Charles was missing and began a search for him down towards the alley. A gate in the middle of the distance led to the moor. Since the day had been wet, Sir Charles' steps were traced to the moor-gate. Barrymore walked down the alley where he found the body. At one point, Sir Charles' footprints became altered; after the moor-gate, the prints appeared as if he had been walking on his toes.

"No signs of struggle were on his body, but his face was so twisted out of shape, Dr. Mortimer almost could not recognize him. Sir Charles' face was twisted as if someone had decided to tickle him into a fit of laughter so painful that he had died. An examination proved death was caused by heart exhaustion. Mr. Henry Baskerville, the son of Sir Charles' younger brother, will live at Baskerville Hall." Dr. Mortimer finished reading.

"You have given me the public facts; now let me have the private facts if there are any." Holmes' face showed no emotion.

"I do know more than I have told so far, but I thought it best not to tell everything. I thought no one would live at Baskerville Hall if all were told. Sir Charles' death does not tickle your mind and it brings me fear." Mortimer told us more.

"Lately, he seemed nervous, strained. He took this legend deeply to heart. He was certain something horrible hung over his family. A presence haunted him. Sometimes he would ask me if I had ever seen a strange creature or heard a hound's baying.

"About three weeks before his death, I drove up to his house one evening. As I came to greet him in his hall door, I saw he was staring over my shoulder. His face was an emotion of awful fear. Turning around quickly I saw a shadow, a hasty sight of something which looked like a large, black calf running down the drive. Sir Charles was very upset. That evening he told me about the Baskerville legend. I thought the story ordinary then; now I believe it has led to his death.

"I told him to visit London for a brief time. A few months away from Baskerville Hall, and its legend of blood, would be an advantage to his health.

"On the night of his death, when Barrymore sent Perkins the horse-keeper to me, I checked all the facts. I looked through the Yew Alley and walked the same footsteps Sir Charles had walked earlier that night. I saw the moor-gate where he had stopped, and I even examined his body. He lay on his face; fingers like claws dug into the ground; a face twisted in a state of fixed pain. Barrymore stated at the hearing there were no footprints near the body. I saw footprints a little distance from the body."

"Footprints?" Holmes asked with interest.

"Yes, footprints."

"A man or a woman's?" Holmes' eyes glowed.

"Mr. Holmes," Dr. Mortimer looked sad, "the footprints of a huge hound."

"You saw this?"

"Clearly."

"Are there large sheep dogs on the moor?"

"No doubt, Mr. Holmes, but this was no sheep dog."

"What sort of night was it?"

"Damp, cold, wet."

"What is the alley like?"

"There are twelve-foot high bushes and a walk eight feet wide in the middle. Between the bushes and the walk is a strip of grass six feet wide on either side. A gate leads to the moor."

"Are there any other openings?"

"None."

"Dr. Mortimer, this is important. Where were the marks you saw, on the path or on the grass?"

"No marks could show on the grass."

"Were they on the same side of the path as the moor-gate?"

"Yes."

"How high was the moor-gate and was it closed?"

"It is about four feet high and it was closed with a strong lock."

"Then anyone could get over it. Were there any marks by the moor-gate?"

"No marks. But I could tell that Sir Charles' cigar had dropped twice."

"Excellent! You do check things."

"Mr. Holmes, the hound, the Power of Evil waits. Think about the legend I have just told you."

"Do you believe in the hound, this Power of Evil, Dr. Mortimer?"

"What I know, Mr. Holmes, is that three people saw a 'thing' before Sir Charles' death, and now Sir Henry will arrive this very afternoon."

The Death of Sir Charles Baskerville

COMPREHENSION CHECK

Choose the best answer.

1. Each evening after dinner, Sir Charles Baskerville would
   ___ a. play games.
   ___ b. read.
   ___ c. go to sleep.
   ___ d. take a walk.

2. First, Sir Charles went out. Then, Barrymore searched for him. Next,
   ___ a. Barrymore found Sir Charles dead.
   ___ b. Barrymore began to worry.
   ___ c. Henry Baskerville came.
   ___ d. Mortimer saw the hound's shadow.

3. The examination showed that Sir Charles died because
   ___ a. the hound attacked him.
   ___ b. he fell.
   ___ c. someone killed him.
   ___ d. his heart gave out.

4. Sir Charles thought that the animal he and Mortimer saw running down the drive was
   ___ a. a large black calf.
   ___ b. the hound of the Baskerville legend.
   ___ c. just a shadow.
   ___ d. a large sheep-dog.

5. The footprints that Mortimer saw near Sir Charles' body were made by
   ___ a. a man.
   ___ b. a woman.
   ___ c. a hound.
   ___ d. Barrymore.

6. After hearing Mortimer's story, Holmes
   ___ a. said he believed it.
   ___ b. said he didn't believe it.
   ___ c. laughed at the idea.
   ___ d. asked many questions.

7. Mortimer could tell that Sir Charles had stood by the gate for five or ten minutes because
   ___ a. he saw footprints there.
   ___ b. he saw cigar ashes on the ground.
   ___ c. he saw marks on the grass.
   ___ d. he knew what time Sir Charles left the house.

8. Mortimer is afraid that the hound of the Baskerville legend
   ___ a. is not real.
   ___ b. will scare Sherlock Holmes.
   ___ c. had something to do with Sir Charles' death.
   ___ d. will kill them all.

9. Another name for this story could be
   ___ a. "Another Strange Death."
   ___ b. "The Locked Gate."
   ___ c. "Sir Charles and His Friends."
   ___ d. "Barrymore the Butler."

10. This story is mainly about
    ___ a. who Sir Charles was.
    ___ b. how Sir Charles lived.
    ___ c. how Sir Charles died.
    ___ d. when Sir Charles became ill.

Check your answers with the key on page 67.

The Death of Sir Charles Baskerville

VOCABULARY CHECK

advantage	afterward	humor	lack	librarian	tickle

I. Sentences to Finish

The six key words are scrambled. Unscramble them and use them to complete the sentences.

ruhom   1.   We brought Steve a book of _____ to cheer him up.

blaarriin   2.   The _____ suggested several books for us to choose from.

tangeadav   3.   It is an _____ to live in a cold climate if you like to ski.

tarfardew   4.   Laura laughed when Jill fell, but _____ , she was sorry.

leckit   5.   Carl tries hard not to laugh when people _____ him.

kalc   6.   The crops are failing because they _____ rain.

II. Finish the Story

Use the key words from the box above to fill in the spaces in the story so that it makes sense.

Mark found a funny book in the _____ section of the library. Reading it, he

began to laugh as much as he does when you _____ him. Of course, the

_____ had to ask him to be quiet. But _____ , she told him

that it is an _____ in life to enjoy a good laugh. She said that he had a gift that

many people _____ .

Check your answers with the key on page 69.

The Heir

PREPARATION

Key Words

exhausted	(eg zô′ stid)	very tired; used up *Frank was exhausted after a day of hard work.*
knob	(nob)	a handle on a door or drawer *It is hard to open a drawer when its knob is loose.*
maple	(mā′ pəl)	wood of the maple tree *The chair was made of maple.*
Mister	(mis′ tər)	a title used before a man's name *Martin learned that his boss liked to be called Mister Riley.*
sofa	(sō′ fə)	a long, soft seat that has a back and arms *Sally was sitting on the sofa when she fell asleep.*
widow	(wid′ ō)	a woman whose husband has died and who has not married again *When Mama became a widow, she wore black clothes.*

The Heir

Necessary Words

heir	(ãr)	one who will receive another person's property after the person's death *As heir to the throne, he would be king some day.*
investigation	(in ves tega' shen)	a detailed study of things and events *When the investigation was complete, the company was cleared of any wrongdoing.*
supernatural	(sü per nach'er el)	beyond what is natural *A ghost is said to be supernatural.*

People

Sir Henry Baskerville   is the heir to the Baskerville estate. He intends to live in Baskerville Hall.

The Heir

Sir Henry Baskerville shows Sherlock Holmes a strange letter that he received at his Hotel and they discuss an unusual happening.

Preview: 1. Read the name of the story.
2. Look at the picture.
3. Read the sentence under the picture.
4. Read the first three paragraphs of the story.
5. Then answer the following question.

You learned from your preview that
___ a. Holmes was not interested in the case.
___ b. Sir Henry Baskerville might be in danger.
___ c. Mortimer's life was in danger.
___ d. Holmes intended to help Mortimer.

Turn to the Comprehension Check on page 22 for the right answer.

Now read the story.

Read to find out how the Baskerville legend will effect Sir Henry.

The Heir

"Dr. Mortimer," began Holmes, "thus far, I have done investigations of only those things that actually exist in this world. You must admit that the footmarks found near Sir Charles' body were indeed real enough."

By this time, Dr. Mortimer looked quite exhausted and worried. Holmes leaned forward in his chair. "Tell me, Dr. Mortimer," said Holmes, "why did you come for help?"

"I hoped," Dr. Mortimer began, "that you would advise me as to what to do about Sir Henry Baskerville. Sir Henry arrives at the Waterloo Train Station in one hour and fifteen minutes. He is the heir to the Baskerville fortune, and given the events of sir Charles' death, I fear for his life."

I was sitting on the sofa nervously tapping my fingers on the small maple table which was next to me. Finally, I asked, "Did Sir Charles leave a widow?"

Dr. Mortimer turned towards me suddenly. "No, Dr. Watson, there is no widow; Sir Charles never remarried. As far as I know, there are no other heirs except Sir Henry. All other family members have long since died. This includes Rodger Baskerville who was the black sheep of the family. They tell me Rodger Baskerville looked very much like the evil Hugo Baskerville, as seen in a family picture. But now, Mister Holmes, what shall I do about Sir Henry?"

"It will take me twenty-four hours to make up my mind about this matter," Holmes began. "I suggest, Dr. Mortimer, that you go and meet Sir Henry at the train station. Then tomorrow at ten o'clock call upon me and bring Sir Henry Baskerville with you."

"Thank you, Mister Holmes," Dr. Mortimer said as he rose to his feet. As our visitor left, I held the knob of the large maple door. I knew it was very important for my friend Holmes to be alone to study the problem in detail, so I left him and went to my club.

Early the next morning, I came back to Baker Street. I found Holmes curled up in an armchair smoking his pipe. There were rolls of paper all around him.

"What have you been doing?" I asked, as I made myself comfortable on the sofa.

"I have been to Devonshire," Holmes began, then quickly added, "in spirit, that is. I must say, my dear Watson, that I now know the moor surrounding the Baskerville estate very well, indeed."

It was not long after when Dr. Mortimer, looking quite exhausted, and young Sir Henry Baskerville arrived. Sir Henry was a short and bright-eyed man, about thirty years of age.

"It is strange," Sir Henry said, "but if my friend Dr. Mortimer hadn't come to see you, I surely would have. You see, only this morning I received a most unusual letter at my hotel, the Northumberland." Holmes examined the letter carefully.

"Hm-mm. Someone seems to be very interested in where you go and what you do," Holmes said. He put the open letter on the table.

It read: **"As you value your life or your reason keep away from the moor."** All the words had been cut from a newspaper, except for the word *"moor"* which was printed in ink.

"You must see, Dr. Mortimer, there is nothing supernatural about this letter." Then Holmes turned to Sir Henry and asked, "Has anything else of interest happened to you in London?"

"Why, yes," Sir Henry said somewhat surprised. "One of my boots is missing. I left the pair outside my hotel door last night to be polished, and this morning, one of them was gone.

"Well, it's indeed unusual to have one boot stolen. But I believe it will turn up soon," Holmes replied.

It was at this point that Holmes asked Dr. Mortimer to read the tale of the Baskervilles to Sir Henry and to inform him of the events of Sir Charles' death.

"I have known of the hound since I was a child, but the death of my uncle is frightening. This letter of warning I've received now seems to fit into place," said Sir Henry.

In spite of the danger, Sir Henry was determined to go to the home of his ancestors. Holmes insisted that I accompany Sir Henry and Dr. Mortimer to Baskerville Hall while he attended to some important business in London.

Before Sir Henry left, he asked Holmes and I to lunch with him and Dr. Mortimer at the Northumberland Hotel at two o'clock. Holmes and I agreed.

I held my hand tightly on the knob of the door as Holmes and I watched Dr. Mortimer and Sir Henry walk down the street.

Suddenly, Holmes cried, "Quickly Watson, we must follow them!"

Holmes and I followed on foot at a safe distance from Sir Henry and Dr. Mortimer; we did not wish to be noticed. A short time later, Holmes cried out, "There's our man. Let's get him!"

I turned to see Holmes rush towards a cab. A man with a thick, dark, bushy beard poked his head out of the cab, then screamed at the driver to pull away quickly. Holmes looked for another cab in which to follow, but there was none to be found.

"What bad luck," Holmes shouted. "The man in that cab has been following Sir Henry the whole time, escaping his notice. Most likely, he has been watching Sir Henry closely since Sir Henry arrived in London. And now, not only has this person escaped us, but worse still, I have made myself known to him."

The Heir

COMPREHENSION CHECK

Preview Answer:
b.   Sir Henry Baskerville might be in danger.

Choose the best answer.

1. Dr. Mortimer told Holmes that
    —— a. Sir Henry had a wife.
    —— b. Rodger Baskerville was still living.
    —— c. Sir Henry was the only living Baskerville.
    —— d. there were many Baskervilles still living.

②. The rolls of paper that Watson saw in Holmes' apartment were
    —— a. maps of the area near the Baskerville home.
    —— b. letters to Sir Henry Baskerville.
    —— c. family pictures.
    —— d. candy wrappers.

3. Sir Henry Baskerville was
    —— a. short and bright-eyed.
    —— b. tall and handsome.
    —— c. short and thin.
    —— d. fat and jolly.

④. First, Sir Henry showed Holmes the letter. Then he told about the missing boot. Next,
    —— a. Sir Henry asked Holmes and Watson to lunch.
    —— b. Sir Henry went back to his hotel.
    —— c. Watson went to his club.
    —— d. Dr. Mortimer told Sir Henry about the hound.

5. Most of the words of the letter that Sir Henry received
    —— a. made no sense.
    —— b. were printed in ink.
    —— c. were written in crayon.
    —— d. had been cut from a newspaper.

6. The letter warned Sir Henry to
    —— a. leave his hotel.
    —— b. keep away from the moor.
    —— c. tell Holmes nothing.
    —— d. go home right away.

7. Holmes said that the man with the dark beard
    —— a. was an old friend of his.
    —— b. had been following Sir Henry.
    —— c. should meet Sir Henry at the train station.
    —— d. had taken Sir Henry's boot.

8. Sherlock Holmes was unhappy because the man with the beard
    —— a. took the wrong cab.
    —— b. moved too slowly.
    —— c. had seen Holmes.
    —— d. argued with him.

⑨. Another name for this story could be
    —— a. "Sir Henry."
    —— b. "A Long Journey."
    —— c. "At the Hotel."
    —— d. "A Good Sign."

⑩. This story is mainly about
    —— a. a strange letter.
    —— b. some unusual happenings.
    —— c. Sir Henry's home.
    —— d. life in London.

Check your answers with the key on page 67.

The Heir

VOCABULARY CHECK

exhausted	knob	maple	Mister	sofa	widow

I. Sentences to Finish

Fill in the blank in each sentence with the correct key word from the box above.

1. When a man dies, he may leave everything to his _____ .

2. Jenny chose _____ furniture for her new room.

3. My neighbor just became a doctor, but sometimes I still call him _____ Webster by mistake.

4. The runners were _____ after the big race.

5. My brother and I sat on the _____ to watch television.

6. Mike turned the _____ quietly and slipped into the room.

II. Crossword Puzzle

Now complete the puzzle with the words you wrote in the blanks. When you are finished, the letters in the shaded boxes will spell the name of someone in the story.

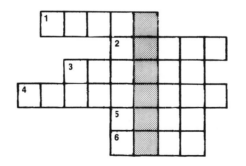

Check your answers with the key on page 69.

Baskerville Hall

PREPARATION

Key Words

attract	(ə trakt′)	cause people or objects to come nearer; win the attention of *Magnets attract iron.*
connect	(kə nəkt′)	join one thing to another *We must connect the lamp cord to the electricity.*
convince	(kən vins′)	make someone believe something *Harry wanted to convince Ed that their team would win.*
exhaust	(eg zôst′)	use up; tire very much *The lost campers will exhaust their food supply in two days.*
expedition	(ek spə dish′ ən)	a trip taken for a special reason *An expedition to the jungle was planned.*
interval	(in′ tər vəl)	a period of time between; pause *After an interval of ten minutes, the second act of the play began.*

Baskerville Hall

Necessary Words

leads	(lēds)	hints to follow *There were three leads for the police to follow in the murder case.*
pounds	(pounds)	unit of British money *I bought a coat in England which cost two hundred pounds.*
telegram	(tel'ə gram)	a telegraph message *She received a telegram that told her to report to work on a London newspaper.*

Baskerville Hall

Holmes questioned the cab driver about the passenger that had been in his cab that morning.

Preview: 1. Read the name of the story.
2. Look at the picture.
3. Read the sentence under the picture.
4. Read the first three paragraphs of the story.
5. Then answer the following question.

You learned from your preview that
____ a.   the man who followed Sir Henry made no mistakes.
____ b.   Holmes thought the bearded man was a cab driver.
____ c.   the man who followed Sir Henry made one mistake.
____ d.   Holmes knows the name of the man who followed Sir Henry.

Turn to the Comprehension Check on page 28 for the right answer.

Now read the story.

Read to find out how Watson goes about trying to discover who is following Sir Henry.

Baskerville Hall

"Well, it is certain from what we have heard that Baskerville has been very closely followed since his arrival in town," said Holmes, "or how else could it be known so quickly that it was the Northumberland Hotel which he had chosen? We are dealing with a smart man, Watson. By taking a cab, he could easily watch Sir Henry and Mortimer or go past them quickly if he should be discovered. And if Sir Henry and Dr. Mortimer were to take a cab, he could follow them quietly and remain unnoticed. But his method has one problem."

"It puts him in the power of the cabman," I said.

"Exactly."

"What a pity we did not get the number."

"My dear Watson, clumsy as I have been, you surely do not think that I forgot the number? Our man is 2704, but that is of no use to us for the moment. I suggest we go to the Bond Street picture exhibit and then to lunch at the Northumberland with Sir Henry and Dr. Mortimer."

For an interval of two hours, Holmes talked of nothing but art. Then we went to the Northumberland Hotel. As we turned to walk down the hall, we came upon Sir Henry Baskerville himself. His face was red with anger. He held an old, dusty boot in one of his hands. After an interval of about a minute, he was able to speak.

"Now my old black boot is missing," Sir Henry shouted. "You cannot convince me that someone did not steal one of my brown boots last night. Now, they have taken one of my black boots. What do you think of all this?"

Holmes looked at Sir Henry and replied, "Well, I don't understand it all yet, but we have several threads to follow and one of them must connect us to the person or persons who wish you harm."

After lunch we all went to a private sitting room.

"I will go to Baskerville Hall at the end of the week," Sir Henry announced.

"On the whole," Holmes said carefully, "I think your decision is a wise one. I am convinced you are being followed in London. You and Dr. Mortimer were followed this morning when you left my house."

Dr. Mortimer shouted, "Followed! By whom?"

"That, unfortunately, I cannot tell you until I have time to exhaust all the leads we now have, but tell me, Dr. Mortimer, do you know of any man in Devonshire with a full, black beard?"

"Why, yes," Dr. Mortimer replied, "Barrymore has a full black beard. He was Sir Charles' butler, and he is still in charge of Baskerville Hall."

Holmes became excited. "We must find out if he could be in London. I will send Barrymore a telegram to be delivered to him personally. If Barrymore is not there, I will request that the telegram be returned to Sir Henry Baskerville, at the Northumberland Hotel."

"Barrymore and his family have been in charge of looking after Baskerville Hall for generations," said Dr. Mortimer.

"Did Barrymore profit at all by Sir Charles' will?" Holmes interrupted.

Dr. Mortimer calmly replied, "He and his wife received five hundred pounds each."

"Then how much money remains in Sir Charles' estate?" Holmes asked.

"Seven hundred and forty thousand pounds," was Dr. Mortimer's reply.

"I had no idea such a large sum was involved," Holmes said with raised eyebrows. "I agree with you, Sir Henry, that you should go to Baskerville Hall. But I must insist that Dr. Watson accompany you and Dr. Mortimer on your expedition. I must remain in London to take care of some important business."

I agreed with pleasure to accompany Sir Henry and Dr. Mortimer. The adventure surrounding this entire matter was enough to attract me to Baskerville Hall.

That evening Holmes received a telegram from Sir Henry which stated that Barrymore had himself accepted the telegram Holmes had sent. This seemed to prove that Barrymore was indeed at Baskerville Hall. Not long after this information arrived, there was a ring at the bell.

A rough-looking fellow stood at the door. "I'm number 2704. I understand you were asking about me," he said.

Holmes assured the man that he had nothing bad to connect to him. Holmes just wanted some information.

"Please tell me about the man who was attracted to where I live and who paid you to let him watch this house, then to follow two gentlemen who left here this morning." Holmes was exhausting the last thread of a lead to follow.

The cabman looked very surprised and said, "The truth is, that the gentleman in my cab was a detective and he didn't want me to talk about him."

"Did he mention his name?" Holmes asked.

"It was Sherlock Holmes," the cabman answered proudly.

Holmes burst into laughter saying, "And can you describe this Sherlock Holmes?"

"He is about forty years old, two or three inches shorter than you and he had a black beard and a pale face. That's all I remember."

"Well, thank you," Holmes said as he slipped some money into the man's hand, "and good night."

After the cabman had gone, Holmes turned to me with a very serious expression on his face. "We are dealing with a very dangerous man, Watson. I am afraid to send you on this expedition to Baskerville Hall." He paused for a moment and then added, "I'll be happy when you return safely here to Baker Street."

Baskerville Hall

COMPREHENSION CHECK

Choose the best answer.

1. First, Holmes and Watson went to an art exhibit. Then, they went to the Northumberland Hotel. Next,
   ___ a. they had lunch with Sir Henry and Dr. Mortimer.
   ___ b. a man came to the door.
   ___ c. Holmes received a telegram.
   ___ d. Holmes told Watson the cab number.

2. Sir Henry's face was red with anger because
   ___ a. someone was following him.
   ___ b. another of his boots was missing.
   ___ c. Holmes and Watson were late for lunch.
   ___ d. his boots were dusty.

3. Dr. Mortimer said that Barrymore, the butler of Baskerville Hall,
   ___ a. had no money.
   ___ b. was being followed.
   ___ c. now lived at the Northumberland Hotel.
   ___ d. had a full, black beard.

4. Holmes sent Barrymore a telegram to
   ___ a. invite Barrymore to lunch.
   ___ b. tell Barrymore what train Watson would be on.
   ___ c. find out if Barrymore could be in London.
   ___ d. tell Barrymore who was following Sir Henry.

5. Holmes suspected that Barrymore was
   ___ a. the man who had followed Sir Henry.
   ___ b. a cab driver.
   ___ c. a spy.
   ___ d. too clever for Holmes to catch.

6. The fact that Barrymore accepted the telegram proved that he was
   ___ a. the man who had followed Sir Henry.
   ___ b. in London.
   ___ c. at Baskerville Hall.
   ___ d. trying to trick Holmes.

7. The cab driver made Holmes laugh by telling him that the man with the beard
   ___ a. was about forty years old.
   ___ b. didn't want the driver to talk about him.
   ___ c. was named Dr. Watson.
   ___ d. was named Sherlock Holmes.

8. Holmes was sorry he had to send Watson to Baskerville Hall because
   ___ a. Watson did all the work.
   ___ b. Watson didn't like trains.
   ___ c. Holmes was afraid there would be danger.
   ___ d. Baskerville Hall was so far away.

9. Another name for this story could be
   ___ a. "Everything Becomes Clear."
   ___ b. "A Great Battle."
   ___ c. "Whispers at Midnight."
   ___ d. "More Surprises."

10. This story is mainly about
    ___ a. leads that don't go anywhere.
    ___ b. the power of money.
    ___ c. sending telegrams.
    ___ d. Sir Henry's courage.

Check your answers with the key on page 67.

Baskerville Hall

VOCABULARY CHECK

attract	connect	convince	exhaust	expedition	interval

I.   Sentences to Finish

Fill in the blank in each sentence with the correct key word from the box above.

1. Ted knows better than to _____ his strength early in the race.

2. To reach the garden, we'll have to _____ another hose to this one.

3. A marching band put on a show in the _____ between the first half and the second half of the game.

4. The men packed supplies for their _____ to the North Pole.

5. Crumbs on the floor will _____ ants .

6. The salesman tried to _____ us that we needed a new car.

II.   Crossword

Now complete the puzzle with the words you wrote in the blanks.

Check your answers with the key on page 70.

People of the Moor

PREPARATION

Key Words

chilly (chil′ ē) unpleasantly cool; rather cold
Tom felt chilly when he went outside without his coat.

froze (frōz) became ice; became very cold
Because the temperatures were so low last winter, the lake froze.

knelt (nelt) bent or rested on the knee
The old man knelt before the king.

shudder (shud′ ər) tremble with horror, fear, or cold
Jane began to shudder as she watched the scary movie.

stubborn (stub′ ərn) refuses to give in
My sister is so stubborn, she did not wear her raincoat even though it was raining.

toboggan (tə bog′ ən) a long, flat-bottomed sled
Four boys sat on the toboggan which slid quickly down the hill.

People of the Moor

Necessary Words

mansion   (man′ shən)   a large house with many rooms
The mansion had a fireplace in every room.

prehistoric   (prē hi stôr′ ik)   the time before recorded history
Cavemen lived on Earth in prehistoric times.

quicksand   (kwik′ sand)   wet sand into which living things will sink and die
The horse fell into the quicksand and could not escape.

People

Stapleton   is a neighbor of the Baskervilles who lives at Merripit House.

Places

Grimpen Mire   is a section of the moor covered with areas of wet, soft ground.

People of the Moor

While Watson was walking near the moor, a man named Stapleton approached him and began asking questions about Sherlock Holmes.

Preview: 1. Read the name of the story.
2. Look at the picture.
3. Read the sentence under the picture.
4. Read the first two paragraphs of the story.
5. Then answer the following question.

You learned from your preview that
____ a. a soldier captured Sir Henry and the others.
____ b. Sherlock Holmes went to Devonshire.
____ c. Sir Henry didn't like the people of the moor.
____ d. a murderer was loose in the moor.

Turn to the Comprehension Check on page 34 for the right answer.

Now read the story.

Read to find out how Watson comes to hear the baying of the hound of the Baskervilles.

People of the Moor

On the given day, Sir Henry, Dr. Mortimer and I arrived in Devonshire. It was a chilly morning. I began to shudder as I watched the train pull away from the station.

A carriage was waiting to take us to Sir Henry's estate. Our carriage ride through the country was pleasant. We were moving as quickly and smoothly as a toboggan moves down a snowy hill, when suddenly our carriage stopped with a jerk. A soldier on horseback was blocking our path. He informed us to proceed with care. There was a dangerous murderer named Selden loose on the moor. This information made me even more uneasy. I shuddered at the thought of a hound and a murderer loose on the moor. I tried to keep in mind that Holmes wanted me to gather facts. I was to make him aware of any new information about the death of Sir Charles. He also wanted to know how Sir Henry felt about the people of the moor and how they felt about him.

We finally arrived at Baskerville Hall. As I stepped out of the carriage, the chilly wind blew even harder. My feet froze to the ground as I looked at the cold and frightening stone mansion.

"Welcome, Sir Henry! Welcome to Baskerville Hall!" called Barrymore and his wife. Barrymore himself was a fine figure of a servant, tall and handsome, with a dark, thick beard.

The great hall of the mansion was lit by a cheery, crackling fire, but dinner was served in the huge, gloomy dining room. That stubborn, chilling fear continued to race through my body during the entire meal. It was with relief that I retired to my more modern and cheerful bedroom, which had a splendid view of the moor.

Although I looked forward to a peaceful night, the silence was suddenly broken by the pitiful sound of a woman sobbing somewhere in the house. The crying froze my senses in a state of extreme watchfulness. I rose from my bed and knelt by the bedroom door. I continued to listen for anything else which might occur, but there was only the sobbing. I knelt by the door for some twenty minutes, listening carefully.

It was after breakfast the next morning that I accidentally met Mrs. Barrymore in a hallway. One look at her face told me she had been crying.

Because Sir Henry was busy examining many papers that morning, I set out on a four-mile walk along the border of the moor. My first stop was at the office of the postmaster. I asked if Holmes' telegram from London had been delivered directly into Barrymore's hands. I learned that it had been given to Mrs. Barrymore, instead. She had said that her husband was very busy at the moment. With this information, there was now no proof that Barrymore had not been in London during the time in question. I wished that Holmes were with me.

I left the postmaster and walked down the long, sloping road next to the moor. I was just beginning to imagine how fine this road might be in winter for a toboggan run. Suddenly, I heard someone running behind me and calling my name. I thought at first it was Dr. Mortimer, but when I turned, I saw a small, slim, blonde-haired man. He was about thirty-five years of age, and he was dressed in a gray suit and a straw hat.

"You must be Dr. Watson," the stranger exclaimed breathlessly. "I am Stapleton of Merripit House. My friend Dr. Mortimer told me you were here. Tell me, how is Sir Henry?"

"He is well," I replied.

"The fame of your friend Mr. Sherlock Holmes and that of yourself is well known here, Dr. Watson. I am curious about what Mr. Holmes thinks of this whole Baskerville matter."

"I am afraid that I cannot answer that question," I replied somewhat surprised, but a quick glance at Stapleton's calm face told me that he had not wanted to surprise me.

"May I ask if Mr. Holmes will honor us with a visit himself?" Stapleton asked.

"He cannot leave town at present because of other cases."

"What a pity! Perhaps he could have helped explain what has been happening here," said Stapleton. "But come now, let me show you the moor. It contains so many secrets. I study nature and there are few men who know their way around the moor as well as I do. There is an incredible variety of insect and plant life here. For example, over there is the great Grimpen Mire. Many men and animals have perished in its quicksand, but I know my way around it. Also, in the center of that hillside, there still stands ancient stone huts which were built by prehistoric man."

I was listening with interest as he described the moor, when suddenly, a long, sad moaning sound filled the air. Then, without warning, the moan turned into a loud roar which lasted several seconds and faded once again into a murmur.

"What was that?" I cried.

Stapleton replied slowly as he stared towards Grimpen Mire, "The peasants say that it is the Hound of the Baskervilles."

People of the Moor

COMPREHENSION CHECK

Preview Answer:

d. a murderer was loose on the moor.

Choose the best answer.

1. The three people who arrived at Baskerville Hall were
    ___ a. Sir Henry, Dr. Mortimer, and Sherlock Holmes.
    ___ b. Sir Henry, a soldier, and a man named Selden.
    ___ c. Sir Henry, Dr. Mortimer, and Dr. Watson.
    ___ d. Dr. Mortimer, Barrymore, and Mrs. Barrymore.

2. During dinner, Watson experienced feelings of
    ___ a. illness.
    ___ b. fear.
    ___ c. pity.
    ___ d. surprise.

3. First, Watson heard a woman crying. Then, he saw Mrs. Barrymore in the hall. Next.
    ___ a. Watson met Stapleton.
    ___ b. dinner was served.
    ___ c. Watson went to bed.
    ___ d. Watson spoke to the postmaster.

4. The new information that Watson discovered about the telegram meant that
    ___ a. Barrymore might have been the man who followed Sir Henry.
    ___ b. Mrs. Barrymore had sent a message to Sherlock Holmes.
    ___ c. Sir Henry was not telling the truth.
    ___ d. Watson would have to leave at once.

5. Walking near the moor, Watson met
    ___ a. the hound of the Baskerville legend.
    ___ b. Sir Henry.
    ___ c. a neighbor named Stapleton.
    ___ d. Barrymore.

6. Watson learned that the people who lived near the moor
    ___ a. had never heard about the hound.
    ___ b. were not afraid of the hound.
    ___ c. didn't believe that the hound was real.
    ___ d. believed that the hound was real.

7. A person who said he knew the moor well was
    ___ a. Dr. Watson.
    ___ b. Grimpen Mire.
    ___ c. Stapleton.
    ___ d. the postmaster.

8. The sound that came from the moor
    ___ a. woke Watson from his sleep.
    ___ b. went on for hours.
    ___ c. changed from a moan to a roar.
    ___ d. was not very loud.

9. Another name for this story could be
    ___ a. "A Peaceful Visit."
    ___ b. "In Devonshire."
    ___ c. "Watson's Secret."
    ___ d. "A Long Night."

10. This story is mainly about
    ___ a. Watson's talk with Mrs. Barrymore.
    ___ b. events that puzzle Watson.
    ___ c. taking the train to Devonshire.
    ___ d. insect and plant life on the moor.

Check your answers with the key on page 67.

This page may be reproduced for classroom use.

People of the Moor

VOCABULARY CHECK

chilly	froze	knelt	shudder	stubborn	toboggan

I. Sentences to Finish

Put a check next to the best answer.

1. You might feel <u>chilly</u>
   ___ a. if the day was cool.
   ___ b. if the day was hot.
   ___ c. if you ate too much.

2. You would say the water <u>froze</u>
   ___ a. if there was a lot of rain.
   ___ b. if you fell in.
   ___ c. if it turned to ice.

3. If you <u>knelt</u>,
   ___ a. you would be sitting.
   ___ b. you would be standing.
   ___ c. you would be on your knees.

4. You might <u>shudder</u>
   ___ a. if you were proud.
   ___ b. if you were scared.
   ___ c. if you were curious.

5. You would be <u>stubborn</u>
   ___ a. if you wouldn't listen.
   ___ b. if you got hurt.
   ___ c. if you forgot something.

6. You would use a <u>toboggan</u>
   ___ a. in the grass.
   ___ b. in the snow.
   ___ c. in the house.

II. Finish the Story

Use the key words in the box above to complete the story so that it makes sense.

Tom and Doug took turns pulling the _____ up the hill. The day was

_____ , so they were dressed warmly. They heard a duck quacking. "It got

trapped in the ice when the pond _____ last night," said Doug.

The duck gave a _____ of fear as the two boys _____

beside it. The ice was hard to break, but Tom and Doug were _____ and kept at

it until the duck was free.

Check your answers with the key on page 70.

Dr. Watson's Report

PREPARATION

Key Words

fiord	(fyôrd)	a narrow inlet of the sea bordered by steep cliffs *The harbor at the end of the fiord was crowded with boats.*
funeral	(fyü′ nər əl)	a service held for someone who has died *The funeral was held in the churchyard.*
horizon	(hə rī′ zn)	line where the earth and sky seem to meet *On the western horizon, Lola could see the sunset.*
ivory	(ī′ vər ē)	hard, white, toothlike material from an elephant or a walrus *The ivory statues were carved with great care.*
parka	(pär′ kə)	a jacket with a hood, used for the cold weather *Robin's parka had a fur lining.*
relative	(rel′ ə tiv)	a person who is part of a family *Ron's favorite relative is Aunt Helen.*

Dr. Watson's Report

Necessary Words

convict   (kon′ vikt)   a person who serves time in prison
> *The escaped convict was known to be dangerous.*

developments   (di vel′ əp mənts)   happenings; results
> *The latest developments in the election show that the governor is ahead.*

extraordinary   (ək strôr′ də ner e)   unusual or amazing
> *The ten-year-old pianist showed extraordinary talent.*

People

Beryl Stapleton   is thought to be the sister of Stapleton and lives in Merripit House.

Selden   is an escaped convict living on the moor. He is the brother of Mrs. Barrymore.

Dr. Watson's Report

Miss Stapleton asked Dr. Watson to forget her words of warning, since they were meant for Sir Henry.

Preview: 1. Read the name of the story.
2. Look at the picture.
3. Read the sentence under the picture.
4. Read the first two paragraphs of the story.
5. Then answer the following question.

You learned from your preview that
____ a. Watson and Stapleton ran away.
____ b. Watson was glad to be left alone.
____ c. Stapleton ran off toward the Great Mire.
____ d. Stapleton was attacked by the hound.

Turn to the Comprehension Check on page 40 for the right answer.

Now read the story.

Read to find out about the unusual happenings at Baskerville Hall.

Dr. Watson's Report

No sooner had the sound of the hound faded into the distance, when Stapleton suddenly gave a cry and began chasing after a small moth. He was very quick and disappeared with great speed in the direction of the Grimpen Mire.

In the distance, there was a small inlet surrounded by steep slopes which reminded me of a fiord. I walked towards this fiord and stopped. Then I turned to stare at the horizon. I was left alone on the moor, and the stillness which surrounded me put me in a sad and lonely mood. It was as if I had just attended the funeral of a dear friend or relative. I saw the sun shine brightly along the horizon, yet I felt strangely cold; I wished I had brought my parka to wear on the chilly moor.

Suddenly, I heard the sound of running footsteps approach me from behind. I turned around and saw, to my surprise, a very beautiful woman. She had skin as smooth and pale as ivory and her hair was as dark as the night. She was very excited.

"Go back!" she cried breathlessly. "Go back, and never set foot upon the moor again!"

"Why should I go back?" I asked.

"I cannot explain," she said in a low voice. "Hush, my brother is coming! Not a word of what I have said."

Stapleton had come back to us. He was breathing hard, and he had given up his chase for the moth.

"Hello, Beryl," Stapleton said. "Have you introduced yourselves?"

"Yes, I was just talking to Sir Henry about the moor," his sister said.

"No, no," said I. "My name is Dr. Watson, a humble friend of Sir Henry's."

Miss Stapleton looked very confused and disappointed. Then she very politely invited me to Merripit House where she and her brother lived. I thought it was odd how such a highly educated man and such a beautiful woman could live in such a lonely place as the moor.

I stayed but a short time at Merripit House. As I was about to leave, Stapleton asked if I thought the afternoon would be a good time for him to meet Sir Henry. I told him that I was sure Sir Henry would be delighted. I walked quickly away from Merripit House, as I was eager to get back to my charge. But before I reached the road, I was surprised to see Miss Stapleton waiting for me.

"I have run all the way in order to cut you off, Dr. Watson," said she. "I must be quick or my brother may miss me. I wanted to tell you to forget what I said to you today, as those words were meant for Sir Henry."

"But Sir Henry is a good friend of mine. Tell me, why were you so eager for Sir Henry to return to London?"

Miss Stapleton hesitated. Then she said that it was her belief in the story of the Hound of the Baskervilles which had prompted her to warn Sir Henry about the danger on the moor.

I questioned Miss Stapleton as to why it was important that her brother not overhear her warnings. She replied that it was important to her brother that Sir Henry remain on the moor. This was because he alone could care for the poor of the area; with that statement, she turned quickly and disappeared in the direction of Merripit House.

Over the next few days, Stapleton and his sister did get to meet Sir Henry. Sir Henry and Miss Stapleton began to show an interest in each other. At first, this did seem extraordinary, but then, since Miss Stapleton was so beautiful and interesting, it was not so unusual. I felt that this attraction could develop into love. However, it was also certain that Stapleton disapproved strongly of Sir Henry and Miss Stapleton spending so much time together.

I kept Holmes informed of all these developments by letter, including the progress of the hunt for the escaped convict, Selden. Soon the most interesting and unusual event happened.

I am normally a very sound sleeper, but because I had been on my guard while at Baskerville Hall, I slept very lightly. One night, after everyone in the house had gone to bed, I heard footsteps pass outside my door. I rose and opened my door. Then, as I looked to the left, I saw the long, black shadow of a man who held a candle. It was Barrymore. I waited and then followed him down the long hall. Suddenly, Barrymore turned into an unfurnished and unused room. I saw him crouch by a window and signal with his candle to someone on the moor.

The next morning, I informed Sir Henry of Barrymore's behavior. Immediately, Sir Henry confronted Barrymore with my story. Barrymore was extremely disturbed and angry, but he would not reveal what he had been doing. Even when Sir Henry threatened to fire him, Barrymore still refused to explain his behavior. Suddenly, Mrs. Barrymore appeared at the doorway, looking very pale and upset.

"We must pack our things and leave," Barrymore said to his wife.

"No!" Mrs. Barrymore cried. "I will tell! A relative of mine is on the moor. We take food to him and we signal him when the food is ready."

"Who is this relative?" Sir Henry asked sternly.

Mrs. Barrymore clutched an ivory charm which she wore around her neck and replied, "It is my brother - the escaped convict, Selden."

Dr. Watson's Report

COMPREHENSION CHECK

Choose the best answer.

1. Stapleton's sister ran up to Watson on the moor and told him
    ___ a. never to set foot on the moor again.
    ___ b. the hound was after her.
    ___ c. she was glad he had come to visit.
    ___ d. Barrymore was leaving.

2. When Miss Stapleton first spoke to Watson, she thought he was
    ___ a. her brother.
    ___ b. Sherlock Holmes.
    ___ c. Sir Henry.
    ___ d. very rude.

3. Watson thought it odd that Stapleton could live in such a lonely place because
    ___ a. Miss Stapleton was so friendly.
    ___ b. Miss Stapleton had to work so hard.
    ___ c. Stapleton was so fearful.
    ___ d. Stapleton was highly educated.

4. Miss Stapleton did not want Watson to
    ___ a. visit Merripit House.
    ___ b. tell her brother what she had said.
    ___ c. introduce her to Sir Henry.
    ___ d. leave Merripit House.

5. When Miss Stapleton and Sir Henry met
    ___ a. they hated each other.
    ___ b. she became very upset.
    ___ c. they liked each other.
    ___ d. she ran away.

6. First, Watson saw Barrymore signal with the candle. Then, he told Sir Henry what he had seen. Next,
    ___ a. Mrs. Barrymore appeared.
    ___ b. Watson heard footsteps.
    ___ c. Watson went back to sleep.
    ___ d. Sir Henry spoke to Barrymore.

7. Watson suspected that
    ___ a. Barrymore planned to harm Sir Henry.
    ___ b. Sir Henry planned to harm Barrymore.
    ___ c. Barrymore had lost his mind.
    ___ d. Sir Henry was lost on the moor.

8. Mrs. Barrymore told Watson and Sir Henry that Barrymore had been signaling to
    ___ a. her brother, Stapleton.
    ___ b. Sherlock Holmes.
    ___ c. her brother, Selden.
    ___ d. Miss Stapleton.

9. Another name for this story could be
    ___ a. "A Beautiful Woman."
    ___ b. "News from London."
    ___ c. "A Change of Plans."
    ___ d. "Watson on the Watch."

10. This story is mainly about
    ___ a. Sir Henry's love for Miss Stapleton.
    ___ b. Barrymore's strange behavior.
    ___ c. the things Watson saw and heard.
    ___ d. why people lived near the moor.

Check your answers with the key on page 67.

This page may be reproduced for classroom use.

Dr. Watson's Report

VOCABULARY CHECK

fiord	funeral	horizon	ivory	parka	relative

I. Sentences to Finish

Fill in the blank in each sentence with the correct key word from the box above.

1. My _____ keeps me warm all winter.

2. Far away on the _____ , we could see mountains.

3. Lisa says that her cousin Kris is both a _____ and a friend.

4. When the leader of that country died, our President went to his _____ .

5. The water in the _____ was cold and salty.

6. To save the lives of elephants, some countries have laws against bringing in

    _____ .

II. Word Search

Now find each key word in the box below and draw a circle around it. The words may be printed from left to right, or from top to bottom. One example, that is __not__ a key word, has been done for you.

```
F U N E R A L D
H F I D H T F R
O D V P N H I L
R E L A T I V E
I F R R E Z O V
Z O L F I O R D
O P A R K A Y R
N A D A N G E R
```

Check your answers with the key on page 70.

Death on the Moor

PREPARATION

Key Words

abandon	(ə ban′ dən)	to leave and not return *After the bomb struck, the captain ordered his men to abandon the ship.*
frantic	(fran′ tik)	very excited because of fear or pain *The mother became frantic when her child was lost.*
ignore	(ig nôr′)	to pay no attention to; to neglect *If you ignore the rules of the pool, you won't be allowed to swim.*
panic	(pan′ ik)	a sudden fear causing people to act wildly *The fire in the movie theater caused a panic in the crowd.*
poisonous	(poi′ zn əs)	containing poison; very harmful to life and health *Cleaning liquids can be poisonous if swallowed.*
witness	(wit′ nis)	a person who saw something happen *She was a witness to the crime.* to see something happen

Death on the Moor

Necessary Words

financial   (fə nan shəl,   that which has to do with money
          fi nan′ shəl)   *A banker helps people with* <u>*financial*</u> *matters.*

People

Laura Lyons   is the woman who was supposed to meet Sir Charles at the moor gate on the night of his death.

Death on the Moor

While Watson was examining a stone hut on the moor, he heard footsteps. He could hardly believe what he saw.

> **Preview:** 1. Read the name of the story.
> 2. Look at the picture.
> 3. Read the sentences under the picture.
> 4. Read the first two paragraphs of the story.
> 5. Then answer the following question.
>
> You learned from your preview that
> ____ a. Selden had been captured.
> ____ b. Selden was still on the moor.
> ____ c. Barrymore wanted Selden to be captured.
> ____ d. Selden had done nothing wrong.
>
> *Turn to the Comprehension Check on page 46 for the right answer.*

Now read the story.

Read to find out who was living on the moor among the stone huts.

Death on the Moor

Sir Henry and I began to search the moor for Selden. We wanted to bring him to justice. But after several hours on the moor, we decided to abandon our search. Selden was nowhere to be found. Yet Sir Henry could not ignore the fact that Barrymore and his wife had been protecting a criminal.

The next morning, Sir Henry had another talk with Barrymore. During the conversation, Barrymore gave his word that he would prevent Selden from harming anyone until he escaped to South America. It was then that Sir Henry decided to abandon his search for Selden. Sir Henry even took it upon himself to give some of his old clothing to Selden to aid in his escape.

"Thank you, Sir Henry," Barrymore said with relief. "You've been so good to us that I feel I should not ignore your kindness." Barrymore hesitated. "Sir Henry, I know something about Sir Charles' death which I learned after the official report was issued."

"What, then?" Sir Henry said as he and I both rose to our feet. "Were you a witness to the murder?"

"No, but I do know why he was at the moor-gate at that hour. He was to meet a woman who signed her name with the letters L.L. I know from this scrap of a letter my wife found in Sir Charles' study weeks after his death. It was written in a woman's hand and the ending of the letter read: 'Please, please, be at the gate by ten o'clock. L.L.' I remember delivering one letter to Sir Charles on the day of his death. It was written by the same woman and it was sent from Coombe Tracey."

Over the next several days, I did my own investigation to discover who this L.L. might be. It was Dr. Mortimer who told me that there was a Laura Lyons living in Coombe Tracey. This Laura Lyons had apparently been deserted by her husband and now earned a small living from a typewriting business.

Soon after, I learned from Barrymore that there was a strange man living on the moor among the stone huts. Selden had told Barrymore about this man.

I decided to investigate Laura Lyons first. I had no difficulty locating her in her room, seated at her typewriter. She was a very beautiful woman, but there was a hardness in her expression. She said she was indeed a friend of Sir Charles. She said he had been kind to her, but when I mentioned the strange note to sir Charles signed L.L., she rose to her feet and became frantic. She began to panic.

When I told her that I had no desire to cause her trouble, she became calm and began to answer my questions.

"My friend Mr. Stapleton had told Sir Charles of my unfortunate financial situation because Sir Charles was known for helping the people of the moor," she said.

"But why did you write that letter to Sir Charles on the day he died?" I asked.

Laura Lyons looked very pale and frantic once more. Then she somehow got control over herself and did not panic.

"It was important that I see him before he left for London because he was to be away for several months."

"Well, what happened when you got there?"

"I never went," she replied.

I was amazed; I questioned her further but could get nowhere.

My next stop was the stone huts. The air and mystery surrounding these huts was poisonous to one. I examined each hut. Then, I discovered one in which someone obviously had been living recently. As I was examining the hut, I heard footsteps. I quickly turned and found a man standing in the doorway. I looked closely; then I sighed with relief, for the man was none other than my friend Sherlock Holmes.

We had much to discuss. Holmes informed me that he had been living on the moor doing his own investigations concerning the Baskerville case, and he had come upon some important information. I told him what I had come to know regarding Laura Lyons. Then Holmes gave me information about this poisonous case which left me cold.

"Did you know that Laura Lyons and Stapleton are very close friends who see each other and write to one another frequently? Also, the lady who passes as Miss Stapleton is really Stapleton's wife."

I gasped and then stared at Holmes in disbelief as he told me the most unusual piece of information.

"It is Stapleton who is the evil figure in this case, and Sir Henry is in extreme danger."

Suddenly, we heard the bloodcurdling scream of a man followed by the horrible baying of a hound.

"The hound!" cried Holmes. "Come, Watson, come! Great Heavens, if we are too late!"

We ran out on the moor and followed the moaning sounds of the hound. Finally, we came to a ridge of rocks which ended in a steep cliff. Below we could see the outline of a man in a horrible, twisted position. It was clear that he had fallen from the cliff. We witnessed a most ghastly sight. The dead, twisted body which we saw in the darkness was the body of Sir Henry Baskerville!

Death on the Moor

COMPREHENSION CHECK

> **Preview Answer:**
>
> b.   Selden was still on the moor.

Choose the best answer.

1. On the night of his death, Sir Charles went to the gate
   ___ a. to meet Sherlock Holmes.
   ___ b. to search for Selden.
   ___ c. because Barrymore sent him there.
   ___ d. to meet a woman.

2. Watson went to Coombe Tracey to question
   ___ a. Barrymore.
   ___ b. Laura Lyons.
   ___ c. Selden.
   ___ d. Stapleton.

3. Watson was amazed to hear that
   ___ a. Selden had escaped.
   ___ b. Laura Lyons was Stapleton's wife.
   ___ c. Barrymore had seen Sir Charles killed.
   ___ d. Laura Lyons asked Sir Charles to meet her, but never went.

4. Sir Charles first heard about Laura Lyons from
   ___ a. Stapleton.
   ___ b. Miss Stapleton.
   ___ c. a mysterious stranger.
   ___ d. Watson.

5. First, Watson learned that a strange man was living on the moor. Then he went to Coombe Tracey. Next,
   ___ a. he learned that Sir Charles received a letter the day he died.
   ___ b. he learned from Dr. Mortimer who L.L. was.
   ___ c. he reported to Sherlock Holmes.
   ___ d. he went to the stone huts.

6. The person whom Watson found living on the moor turned out to be
   ___ a. a killer.
   ___ b. Stapleton.
   ___ c. Sherlock Holmes.
   ___ d. Laura Lyons.

7. Holmes did <u>not</u> tell Watson
   ___ a. that Laura Lyons and Stapleton were friends.
   ___ b. that Sir Henry was safe.
   ___ c. that Miss Stapleton was really Stapleton's wife.
   ___ d. that Stapleton was a bad person.

8. Sir Henry Baskerville fell from the cliff
   ___ a. because the night was so dark.
   ___ b. because the hound was chasing him.
   ___ c. but he was all right afterward.
   ___ d. a long time before Holmes and Watson found him.

9. Another name for this story could be
   ___ a. "The Hound Strikes."
   ___ b. "Safe At Home."
   ___ c. "A Tough Struggle."
   ___ d. "Holmes in Danger."

10. This story is mainly about
    ___ a. why you should be careful on a moor.
    ___ b. searching for an escaped prisoner.
    ___ c. the facts surrounding two deaths.
    ___ d. living in stone huts.

Check your answers with the key on page 67.

Death on the Moor

VOCABULARY CHECK

abandon	frantic	ignore	panic	poisonous	witness

I. Sentences to Finish

Fill in the blank in each sentence with the correct key word from the box above.

1. The children remained calm and didn't _____ when the lights went out.

2. Tim was thrilled to _____ the launch of the space station.

3. They had to _____ their car when it broke down in the desert.

4. Some medicines can be _____ if you take too much.

5. The poor baby was _____ when her finger was caught in the door.

6. It is dangerous to _____ a red light.

II. Crossword Puzzle

Use the key words to complete the puzzle.

Across

1. pay no attention to

2. to leave behind

3. harmful to your body

Down

4. a sudden wild fear

5. to see something happen

6. excited because of fear or pain

Check your answers with the key on page 71.

Closing In

PREPARATION

Key Words

atmosphere   (at′ mə sfir)   a feeling surrounding a place
The Sherlock Holmes stories have an atmosphere of mystery.
the air around us

entrance   (en′ trəns)   a door; a place to enter
The entrance to the cave was hidden by bushes.

inspect   (in spekt′)   to look over carefully; examine
The health officer came to inspect the basement.

relax   (ri laks′)   to loosen up; feel freer
I like to relax by taking long walks by myself.

resolution   (rez ə lü′ shən)   firmness of purpose; willpower
I made a resolution to wake up earlier every morning.

suggestion   (səg jes′ chən)   a hint; the smallest showing of feeling
There was a suggestion of a break in his voice.

Closing In

Necessary Words

appointment	(ə point′ mənt)	an agreed time and place to meet *They made an appointment to meet again in a week.*
photographs	(fō′ tə grafs)	pictures taken with a camera *The photographs showed the places and people he had visited on his vacation.*
portrait	(pôr′ trit, pôr′ trat)	a picture painted or taken of a person *The artist captured her lovely smile in the portrait he painted.*
warrant	(wôr′ ənt, wor′ ənt)	a written order giving someone the right to do something, such as make an arrest *Before they could reach the room the police had to show a warrant.*

People

Lestrade	is a famous police officer that Holmes calls to Devonshire.

Closing In

Sherlock Holmes and Dr. Watson meet Police Officer Lestrade at the Coombe Tracey Train Station.

Preview: 1. Read the name of the story.
2. Look at the picture.
3. Read the sentence under the picture.
4. Read the first three paragraphs of the story.
5. Then answer the following question.

You learned from your preview that
___ a. Holmes blamed himself for Sir Henry's death.
___ b. Sir Henry was killed by Selden.
___ c. Sir Henry was not dead after all.
___ d. Sir Henry had a beard.

Turn to the Comprehension Check on page 52 for the right answer.

Now read the story.

Read to find out about Sherlock Holmes' plan.

Closing In

We listened to his screams and yet we were unable to save him! "Stapleton shall answer for this deed," I shouted with resolution.

"I will see to that," Holmes replied. "Sir Charles was frightened to death by the very sight of the beast, and Sir Henry was driven to his end in his wild flight to escape from it! Now, we must prove that there is a link betwen Stapleton and the hound."

We went down to inspect the twisted body of Sir Henry. Suddenly Holmes gave a cry, "This man has a beard! He is not Sir Henry; he is Selden, the convict!"

I remembered that Sir Henry had given his old clothing to Barrymore to help Selden escape. I told this to Holmes. Then I began to relax, secure in the knowledge that Sir Henry was not dead.

"These clothes were the cause of the poor fellow's death," Holmes said with resolution. "It is clear that the hound was following the scent of some article of Sir Henry's, probably the boot which was taken from the hotel. And so the hound ran this man down." There was a suggestion of pity in Holmes' voice.

The tragic death of Selden, the very real presence of the hound, and the evil figure of Stapleton, made the atmosphere of the moor even more frightening.

As I thought of Stapleton, I suddenly recalled with horror that Sir Henry had accepted an invitation from Stapleton to dine at Merripit House the next evening. I, too, had been invited and had accepted. I had told all this to Holmes in my last report. Now, I voiced my fears. To my surprise, Holmes insisted that Sir Henry should go to Merripit House, but I should excuse myself. Holmes planned to lay a trap for Stapleton and, in this way, gather enough evidence against him.

We covered Selden's face with a cloth and left his body on the rocks to be taken away the next morning. We hurried back to Baskerville Hall. As we went through the entrance to the estate, I felt relieved to escape the chilly atmosphere of the moor.

Sir Henry was very pleased to see Holmes. We all had a late supper. During supper, Holmes and I told Sir Henry much, but not all, of what happened on the moor. We avoided any mention of Stapleton or the hound in connection with Selden's death.

After supper, Sir Henry went to his room. It was then that Holmes chanced upon a most amazing piece of information about the Baskerville case.

In the old dining room there hung portraits of members of the Baskerville family. The one hanging near the entrance to the room attracted Holmes. It was the portrait of the wicked Hugo who had started the legend of the Hound of the Baskervilles. Holmes began to inspect the portrait carefully. I, too, gazed at the picture.

Suddenly, I saw what Holmes must have noticed from the start. There was a suggestion of Sir Henry in the face of the evil Hugo. But even more, the face on the canvas was the face of Stapleton himself.

The portrait, painted in 1647, was definitely of Sir Hugo, but the likeness to Stapleton was truly remarkable.

The next morning Holmes was up early. By the time I had finished dressing, he had already begun to make plans to trap Stapleton.

Holmes told Sir Henry that he and I were leaving for London immediately. Sir Henry felt hurt and somewhat frightened by our plans to leave, but Holmes told him that he had nothing to fear if he followed certain directions exactly. Sir Henry relaxed a little and agreed.

Holmes told Sir Henry to dine as planned at the Stapleton's that evening and to tell Stapleton that Holmes and I had returned to London. Holmes also directed Sir Henry to be driven to Merripit House, to send his carriage away, and to walk his usual route back to Baskerville Hall. Holmes insisted that all of this was very important to Sir Henry's safety. Sir Henry agreed to everything. Then Holmes and I left Baskerville Hall for the train station at Coombe Tracey.

At the train station, Holmes received an answer to a telegraph message he had sent earlier that morning. It was from the famous police officer, Lestrade. In his reply, Lestrade said he would arrive at five-forty with a warrant. It was then clear to me that we would not leave Devonshire after all.

First, we paid Laura Lyons a visit. With the aid of photographs and the written word of those who had known the couple, Holmes proved to her that Stapleton and his sister were really husband and wife.

Shaken by this proof, Laura Lyons told us how Stapleton had urged her to write to Sir Charles and arrange to meet him at the gate. She was to ask him for money to secure her divorce so that she and Stapleton could marry. But at the last minute, Stapleton had told her not to keep her appointment. Thus, Sir Charles was to be at the gate alone. Holmes told Laura Lyons that she had the power to stop Stapleton, and that she was lucky to still be alive.

Holmes and I left Laura and went to the train station to await Lestrade's arrival.

Closing In

COMPREHENSION CHECK

Choose the best answer.

1. The hound chased Selden because
    ___ a. Selden hit him.
    ___ b. it was helping the police.
    ___ c. Selden was wearing Sir Henry's clothes.
    ___ d. Selden had a beard.

2. Holmes wanted Sir Henry to
    ___ a. dine at Stapleton's house.
    ___ b. go away at once.
    ___ c. hide on the moor.
    ___ d. stay away from Stapleton.

3. Holmes noticed that the picture of the wicked Hugo Baskerville
    ___ a. was missing from the wall.
    ___ b. looked exactly like Sir Henry.
    ___ c. looked exactly like Stapleton.
    ___ d. was hanging in Merripit House.

4. When Sir Henry heard that Holmes and Watson were leaving, he felt
    ___ a. glad.
    ___ b. angry.
    ___ c. safe.
    ___ d. frightened.

5. Sir Henry was supposed to walk home from Merripit House because
    ___ a. he liked fresh air.
    ___ b. his carriage was broken.
    ___ c. that was part of Holmes' trap.
    ___ d. Holmes thought he needed the exercise.

6. Holmes and Watson left Baskerville Hall to go to
    ___ a. the train station.
    ___ b. Merripit House.
    ___ c. the moor.
    ___ d. a dinner party.

7. First, Holmes received a telegram. Then, he and Watson visited Laura Lyons. Next,
    ___ a. they went to wait for Lestrade.
    ___ b. they hurried to Baskerville Hall.
    ___ c. Holmes sent a telegram to Lestrade.
    ___ d. Sir Henry agreed to follow Holmes' directions.

8. Laura Lyons was lucky to be alive because
    ___ a. she didn't have enough money to buy food.
    ___ b. she knew too much about Stapleton.
    ___ c. the hound was after her.
    ___ d. she was very old.

9. Another name for this story could be
    ___ a. "At the Train Station."
    ___ b. "Setting a Trap."
    ___ c. "A Cold Wind."
    ___ d. "Broken Promises."

10. This story is mainly about
    ___ a. Selden's death.
    ___ b. family pictures.
    ___ c. Lestrade.
    ___ d. Holmes' plan.

Check your answers with the key on page 67.

Closing In

VOCABULARY CHECK

atmosphere	entrance	inspect	relax	resolution	suggestion

I. Sentences to Finish

The key words are scrambled. Unscramble them and use them to complete the sentences.

lexar   1. It feels good to _____ after a hard day.

gusnegosit   2. Cara thought she saw a _____ of a smile on Jason's lips.

ratcenne   3. Our clubhouse has a secret _____ .

penstic   4. Before you buy candy, _____ the wrapper to see that it hasn't been opened.

herometsap   5. We enjoy visiting the Moores because their home has a warm and friendly

_____ .

lionsotrue   6. Alan showed a great deal of _____ in staying with the job until it was done.

II. Matching

Write the letter of the correct meaning from Column B next to the key word in Column A.

Column A

_____ 1. atmosphere

_____ 2. entrance

_____ 3. inspect

_____ 4. relax

_____ 5. resolution

_____ 6. suggestion

Column B

a. to feel more free

b. a hint

c. a door

d. the feeling of a place

e. firmness of purpose

f. examine

Check your answers with the key on page 71.

The Hound of the Baskervilles

PREPARATION

Key Words

crystal   (kris' tl)   something that can be seen through because it is so clear
She could see sea shells through the crystal waters.
a clear mineral or glass

delicate   (del' ə kit)   fine in construction; easily broken
He was careful not to drop the delicate glass statue.

detail   (di tāl', de' tāl)   a very small part
The plan was perfect, down to the last detail.

oxygen   (ok' sə jən)   a colorless gas in the air that living things must breathe in order to live
Animals and plants cannot live without oxygen.

souvenir   (sü və nir')   something given or kept to remember a place visited
He bought a small souvenir to remind him of his vacation.

tourist   (tur' ist)   a person who takes a trip for pleasure
The tourist carried a camera so that she could take pictures of the city.

The Hound of the Baskervilles

Necessary Words

muzzle   (muz′ əl)   the lower part of a dog's head including the nose, mouth and jaws
> *The hound's <u>muzzle</u> was covered with dirt after he buried a bone in the yard.*

paralyzed   (par′ ə līzd)   unable to move
> *She was <u>paralyzed</u> by her fear of height and was unable to climb down the tall ladder.*

The Hound of the Baskervilles

As Holmes, Watson, and Lestrade raced up the path, they saw the huge hound spring upon Sir Henry.

Preview:
1. Read the name of the story.
2. Look at the picture.
3. Read the sentence under the picture.
4. Read the first paragraph of the story.
5. Then answer the following question.

You learned from your preview that
____ a. Holmes was too late to save Sir Henry.
____ b. Lestrade intended to shoot Sir Henry.
____ c. Holmes was putting his plan into action.
____ d. Holmes had changed his mind about Stapleton.

Turn to the Comprehension Check on page 58 for the right answer.

Now read the story.

Read to find out if Sir Henry will escape from the hound.

The Hound of the Baskervilles

Lestrade arrived with a gun in his pocket and soon we were on our way back to the moor. It had grown dark. Holmes asked the carriage driver to let us off some distance before Merripit House. Then Lestrade, Holmes and I walked softly towards the house. We waited motionless outside, hidden behind some rocks. I looked into the dining room window and saw Stapleton and Sir Henry. Sir Henry looked very pale as he listened to Stapleton, who held a delicate, crystal wine glass in his hand. I thought the detail on the crystal was very beautiful. It reminded me of a souvenir I had bought as a tourist in Germany.

Suddenly, I saw Stapleton stand up. He walked out of the dining room and out of the house. He passed so near to us that I held my breath, but soon I had a need for oxygen and gasped for air.

We watched as Stapleton walked to an outhouse and unlocked the door. There was a curious scuffling noise which came from within the small building. Soon Stapleton locked the door and returned to the house.

As we watched and listened, a dense, white fog began to creep slowly towards us. Even with the help of the full moon, I was able to make out few details in the distance.

Finally, we heard the sound of quick footsteps. It was Sir Henry as he passed close by us.

Suddenly, Holmes cried, "Hist! It's coming!" We stared at the cloud of fog which lay ahead. I saw Holmes' lips part in amazement. Then Lestrade yelled in terror. I was breathing heavily, but had to gasp for oxygen when I saw what came out of the fog.

A dreadful shape had sprung out at us. It It was an enormous, coal-black hound, but not such as any living man had seen on earth. Fire burst from the animal's open mouth; its eyes glared, and the hound's muzzle was outlined in a flickering flame. It was a beast out of hell, more savage than anything I had ever seen.

With long leaps, the creature was racing down the track after our friend, Sir Henry. At first, we stood paralyzed with fear. But then Holmes and I recovered our nerve. We both fired at the creature. It gave out a fearful howl, but continued to go after Sir Henry. I could see Sir Henry's pale-white face in the moonlight. His hands were raised in horror. He let out frightful screams as the ghastly hound hunted him down.

We ran up the path and arrived in time to see the beast spring upon Sir Henry, hurl him to the ground, and prepare to tear at his throat.

But in a moment, Holmes had emptied five barrels of his gun into the creature's side. With one last howl, the hound rolled on its back and then fell limp on its side. We rushed to Sir Henry and found, with relief, that his throat was untouched.

"My God!" Sir Henry whispered. "What in heaven's name was it?"

"It's dead, whatever it was," said Holmes. "We've laid the family ghost to rest."

I bent down and touched the beast's glowing muzzle. It was covered with a luminous mixture. We left Sir Henry to rest and rushed back to Merripit House. We searched the house. There was no sign of Stapleton. Suddenly, we heard a faint, moaning sound coming from a locked bedroom. Holmes broke open the door and we rushed into the room. I gasped at what I saw. Tied to a post in the center of the room, was a human figure wrapped in sheets. The delicate features of Mrs. Stapleton's head could be seen at the top. She was bound and gagged.

We quickly freed her.

"Is Sir Henry safe?" she gasped.

"Yes," Holmes replied, "and the hound is dead."

"Thank God," she sighed.

I looked around the room and found that it was filled with moth and butterfly collections, as well as all manner of souvenirs which a tourist might collect during his travels.

Mrs. Stapleton sobbed as she told us how Stapleton had lied to her and mistreated her. When Holmes pressed her to tell us where Stapleton had fled, she quickly identified the one place he was likely to go.

"There is an old tin mine on an island in the heart of Grimpen Mire. It was there that he had kept his hound; he had prepared it as a hiding place for himself as well. Even he could never find his way through the Mire in this fog without being sucked into the quicksand," she added.

The next morning, when the fog had lifted and when Mrs. Stapleton had gained back her strength, she led us through the Mire. There were no footsteps we could follow, and we were in constant danger of being sucked into the quicksand ourselves.

Holmes found Sir Henry's missing black boot, which Stapleton had used to put the hound on Sir Henry's scent, but we never found Stapleton.

"Never yet have we helped to hunt down a more dangerous man than he who is lying yonder," said Holmes, as he swept his arm towards the marsh.

The Hound of the Baskervilles

COMPREHENSION CHECK

Choose the best answer.

1. First, Stapleton walked out of the house. Then, he unlocked a small building. Next,
   ___ a. Lestrade yelled in terror.
   ___ b. Sir Henry left the house.
   ___ c. Holmes, Watson, and Lestrade hid behind some rocks.
   ___ d. Holmes fired his gun at the hound.

2. Holmes began to worry because
   ___ a. the moon was too bright.
   ___ b. Sir Henry was not following directions.
   ___ c. Watson was having trouble breathing.
   ___ d. the night was growing foggy.

3. Sir Henry was attacked by
   ___ a. Stapleton.
   ___ b. a hound that seemed to breathe fire.
   ___ c. a dragon.
   ___ d. a ghost from Stapleton's past.

4. The scuffling noise that was heard when Stapleton unlocked the small building was caused by
   ___ a. the hound.
   ___ b. Stapleton's footsteps.
   ___ c. Watson gasping.
   ___ d. the wind.

5. When Sir Henry was attacked, Holmes
   ___ a. screamed.
   ___ b. shot the hound.
   ___ c. threw him to the ground.
   ___ d. rushed back to the house.

6. The beast's face and mouth glowed because
   ___ a. they were on fire.
   ___ b. the lights were bright.
   ___ c. Watson touched them.
   ___ d. they had a special mixture on them.

7. The figure tied to a post in Stapleton's house was
   ___ a. Stapleton.
   ___ b. Sir Henry.
   ___ c. Mrs. Stapleton.
   ___ d. the hound.

8. Stapleton ran onto the moor and
   ___ a. escaped.
   ___ b. was shot.
   ___ c. died in the quicksand.
   ___ d. was killed by the hound.

9. Another name for this story could be
   ___ a. "The Savage Beast."
   ___ b. "Watson's Wish."
   ___ c. "The Butterfly Collection."
   ___ d. "Dinner at Merripit House."

10. This story is mainly about
    ___ a. the dangers of quicksand.
    ___ b. how Stapleton trained the hound.
    ___ c. the end of the Baskerville legend.
    ___ d. Mrs. Stapleton's sad life.

Check your answers with the key on page 67.

This page may be reproduced for classroom use.

The Hound of the Baskervilles

VOCABULARY CHECK

crystal	delicate	detail	oxygen	souvenir	tourist

I. Sentences to Finish

Fill in the blank in each sentence with the correct key word from the box above.

1. The sparkling ice was _____ clear.

2. There are many exciting things for a _____ to see in this city.

3. The spider's web looked too _____ to catch a fly.

4. Marcie kept a pretty shell as a _____ of her trip to the beach.

5. Mike made holes in the top of the jar so the grasshopper would have enough

   _____ .

6. Instead of just telling what the movie was about, Josh told every _____ of the plot.

II. Crossword Puzzle.

Now use the key words to fill in the puzzle. The letters in the shaded blocks will tell what Sherlock Holmes might say about the Baskerville case.

Down

1. clear enough to see through

2. person on a trip for pleasure

3. easy to break

4. something to remember a place by

5. gas that we breathe

6. a small part

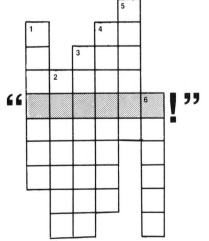

Check your answers with the key on page 71.

The Details of the Case

PREPARATION

Key Words

conscious   (kon′ shəs)   awake; to have knowledge of
> *Bob remained <u>conscious</u> after his fall from the tree.*

dread   (dred)   to fear greatly
> *People in city apartments <u>dread</u> the summer heat.*

fling   (fling)   to hurl; to throw hard
> *Our pitcher can <u>fling</u> a baseball faster than anyone else.*

flip   (flip)   to toss into the air
> *The dancer could <u>flip</u> her partner over her head.*

pressure   (presh′ ər)   continued force
> *The <u>pressure</u> of water in the pipes made them burst.*

rudder   (rud′ ər)   a flat piece of wood or metal used for steering
> *A <u>rudder</u> is used to steer even the largest ship.*

The Details of the Case

People

Rodger Baskerville   is the real name of Jack Stapleton. He is named after his father.

Places

Costa Rica   is a country in Central America, northwest of Panama.

Devonshire   is a county in SW England.

Yorkshire   is a county in NE England.

The Details of the Case

Dr. Watson asked Holmes to explain the details of the Baskerville mystery.

Preview: 1. Read the name of the story.
        2. Look at the picture.
        3. Read the sentence under the picture.
        4. Read the first paragraph of the story.
        5. Then answer the following question.

You learned from your preview that
___ a. the Baskerville mystery is still not solved.
___ b. Holmes already told Watson all the details.
___ c. Watson still didn't know all the details.
___ d. Watson was not really interested in the details.

Turn to the Comprehension Check on page 64 for the right answer.

Now read the story.

Read to find out how Stapleton was connected with the Baskerville Family.

The Details of the Case

It was a chilly and foggy night in November when Holmes and I sat on either side of a blazing fire in his sitting room at Baker Street. Holmes had solved two other cases since the Baskerville affair. I was conscious of the fact that Holmes was in the best of spirits and felt no pressure due to any unsolved case. It was then that I asked him to explain the details of the Baskerville mystery.

"I have spoken with Mrs. Stapleton on two occasions," Holmes began. "She has provided the details to Stapleton's background. The family portrait did not lie, Watson. Stapleton was indeed a Baskerville. He was the son of Rodger Baskerville, who had fled to South America. Rodger Baskerville had not died unmarried. He did in fact, marry and have one child, this fellow, Stapleton, whose real name is the same as his father's. Stapleton married Beryl Garcia, a beauty from Costa Rica. Then, after stealing a large sum of public money, he changed his name to Vandeleur and fled to Yorkshire, England. He attempted to run a school and make a success out of it, but instead, the school's name went from bad to worse. The Vandeleurs then decided to change their name to Stapleton and move to Devonshire. It was on the moor that Stapleton could develop his talent as a naturalist while trying to do away with Sir Charles and Sir Henry. They were the two heirs who stood in the way of his inheriting the Baskerville fortune."

I listened carefully as Holmes continued to talk about the background of this strange man.

"First, Stapleton decided to pass his wife off as his sister. He was prepared to use her as a tool to achieve his ends. He also arranged to live close to Baskerville Hall and to develop a friendship with Sir Charles Baskerville. Stapleton knew that Sir Charles had a weak heart. He also knew that Sir Charles lived in dread of the Baskerville hound.

"Stapleton tried to make his wife form a very close friendship with Sir Charles. But nothing, not even blows, would move her. So, Stapleton used Mrs. Laura Lyons as his tool. Thus, Sir Charles was waiting at the gate on the night of his death because of Mrs. Lyon's letter. But as you know, Stapleton prevented her from keeping the appointment. Instead, he waited outside the gate with the huge, black hound which he had bought and secretly taken to the moor. Angered by its master, the hound raced after Sir Charles, who ran away in terror from this dreaded creature. The hound ran on the grass, thus leaving no tracks. Seeing Sir Charles lying so still, the hound had probably gone near to sniff him. It was then that it left the print that Dr. Mortimer saw.

"As for Mrs. Stapleton and Mrs. Laura Lyons, both women were under Stapleton's influence. Without his love, each felt like a ship without a rudder. Yet each of them came to suspect the man's evil intentions.

"Stapleton's first idea was that he would kill Sir Henry in London. Stapleton forced his wife to go with him to London so he could watch her closely. He imprisoned her in the Mexborough Private Hotel. Then, Stapleton disguised himself in a beard and began to carry out his plans to get rid of Sir Henry. Mrs. Stapleton, who was conscious of the danger to Sir Henry, sent him that letter of warning. Stapleton felt a good deal of pressure when he learned I was on the case. He decided to leave Sir Henry alone in London and go after him with his hound in Devonshire instead.

"It was my game to watch Stapleton, and so I came to live among the stone huts of the moor. By the time you had discovered me, Watson, I had learned much about Stapleton and the whole Baskerville business. But my case against Stapleton was still like a boat without a rudder. I had to catch Stapleton red-handed."

"Yes, and that we did," Watson said.

"We succeeded in completing our case, but at the cost of giving a severe shock to our friend Sir Henry, and driving Stapleton to his death on the moor," Holmes replied. "A long journey will let our friend recover, not only from his frightening experience, but also from his wounded feelings. His love for Mrs. Stapleton was deep and sincere. To him, the saddest part of all was that he should have been tricked by her.

"As for Mrs. Stapleton, she had agreed to her husband's command to pass as his sister. However, she was ready again and again to warn Sir Henry of danger, as long as in so doing, she did not draw attention to her husband."

As I listened to Holmes, I pictured the savage hound that was able to fling Sir Henry to the ground. I pictured also its master who had wanted to flip the coin of fate to achieve his evil ends.

"And now my dear Watson," I heard my friend say, "we have worked very hard for the past several weeks. We should relax for one evening. I have a box for an opera tonight. Might I trouble you to be ready in half an hour, and we can stop at Marcini's for a little dinner on the way."

I smiled at my dear friend, Mr. Sherlock Holmes, and quickly agreed.

The Details of the Case

COMPREHENSION CHECK

Choose the best answer.

1. Stapleton's real name was
    ___ a. Rodger Baskerville.
    ___ b. Lyons.
    ___ c. Costa Rica.
    ___ d. Sir Charles Baskerville.

2. First, the younger Rodger Baskerville stole some money. Then, he changed his name to Vandeleur. Next,
    ___ a. he married Beryl Garcia.
    ___ b. he fled to South America.
    ___ c. he changed his name to Stapleton.
    ___ d. he forced his wife to go to London.

3. Stapleton arranged to live near Sir Charles Baskerville because
    ___ a. he liked Sir Charles.
    ___ b. he had a school there.
    ___ c. his wife liked it there.
    ___ d. he planned to kill Sir Charles.

4. If Sir Charles and Sir Henry both died,
    ___ a. the Baskerville fortune would go to Stapleton.
    ___ b. there would be no Baskervilles left.
    ___ c. Stapleton would lose his two best friends.
    ___ d. it would show that the legend of the hound was true.

5. Stapleton wanted Sir Charles to go to the gate
    ___ a. so Laura Lyons could meet him.
    ___ b. so he could tie him up and beat him.
    ___ c. so he could scare him to death with the hound.
    ___ d. so he would catch cold and die.

6. Stapleton first planned to
    ___ a. kill Sir Henry with a knife.
    ___ b. kill Sir Henry in London.
    ___ c. warn Sir Henry.
    ___ d. keep Sir Henry prisoner.

7. Holmes lived among the stone huts in order to
    ___ a. relax.
    ___ b. hide from the hound.
    ___ c. catch Stapleton.
    ___ d. catch butterflies.

8. Holmes was glad that
    ___ a. Sir Henry had had a bad shock.
    ___ b. Stapleton was dead.
    ___ c. Sir Henry was going on a journey.
    ___ d. Sir Henry was tricked by Mrs. Stapleton.

9. Another name for this story could be
    ___ a. "The Explanation."
    ___ b. "A New Mystery."
    ___ c. "An Evening at the Opera."
    ___ d. "Holmes Hesitates."

10. This story is mainly about
    ___ a. Watson's curiosity.
    ___ b. the facts behind the Baskerville mystery.
    ___ c. the tricks Holmes used to solve mysteries.
    ___ d. plans for the future.

Check your answers with the key on page 67.

This page may be reproduced for classroom use.

The Details of the Case

VOCABULARY CHECK

conscious	dread	fling	flip	pressure	rudder

I. Sentences to Finish

Fill in the blank in each sentence with the correct key word from the box above.

1. It's easy to _____ a ball a foot or two above your head and catch it again.

2. Pete tried to _____ a rock all the way across the river.

3. When Joe got tired of steering, Kathy took over the _____ .

4. The doctor said the patient was _____ and able to speak.

5. When the hurricane struck, we understood why people _____ these huge storms.

6. Firm _____ on the cut soon stopped the blood from flowing.

II. Matching

Draw a line from each word in Column A to its meaning in Column B.

Column A

1. conscious

2. dread

3. fling

4. flip

5. pressure

6. rudder

Column B

a. to toss in the air

b. to fear greatly

c. part to steer with

d. to throw hard

e. awake

f. steady force

Check your answers with the key on page 72.

NOTES

HOW TO
GIVE A
TERRIFIC
PRESENTATION

The WorkSmart Series

HOW TO
GIVE A
TERRIFIC
PRESENTATION

Karen Kalish

amacom

AMERICAN MANAGEMENT ASSOCIATION

THE WORKSMART SERIES

New York • Atlanta • Boston • Chicago • Kansas City • San Francisco • Washington, D.C.
Brussels • Toronto • Mexico City

Library of Congress Cataloging-in-Publication Data

Kalish, Karen.
    How to give a terrific presentation / Karen Kalish.
        p. cm.— (The WorkSmart series)
    Includes bibliographical references.
    ISBN 0-8144-7841-7
    1. Business presentations. I. Title. II. Series.
  HF5718.22.K35 1997
  658.4'52—dc20   96-38791
                                      CIP

Printing number

10   9   8   7   6   5   4

CONTENTS

Make thyself a craftsman in speech,
for thereby thou shalt gain the upper hand.

—Inscription found in a 3,000-year old Egyptian tomb

INTRODUCTION

> If all my talents and powers were to be taken from me by some inscrutable Providence, and I had my choice of keeping but one, I would unhesitatingly ask to be allowed to keep the Power of Speaking, for through it I would quickly recover all the rest.
>
> —**Daniel Webster**

I can remember standing up in fifth grade to make a presentation on Chopin, and when I said that he was a pianist, pronouncing it as if it had only two syllables, the other students broke into gales of laughter. At first I didn't understand what was so funny. Then I was mortified. I never got up to speak in public again until twenty-four years later, when I became a TV reporter, first at the CBS station in Washington, D.C., then at WLS-TV in Chicago.

Since then I have read every book on speechmaking I could find. I've tried every new idea I came across, and discarded those that didn't work. Through trial and error, mostly error, I've found ways to be more dynamic and effective as a speaker, and I've come to love giving speeches and making presentations. It was a good thing, because I kept getting more and more invitations to speak.

I left Chicago and moved back to Washington, D.C., where I was the Washington reporter/producer for *Entertainment Tonight* for a couple of years. I gave up that job to learn about and play the stock market. It was then that my phone started ringing. "I have to give a speech next week; can you help me?" "Can you teach so-and-so how to put a speech together?" I found that I could teach others the many things I'd learned and put into practice. My clients came in psychological wrecks and walked out successful speakers.

One client customarily delivered an angry speech, but after we changed the tone of her presentation, she was successful as a public speaker. Another client, an ex-football player, wanted to continue to talk about football even though he hadn't played for fourteen years! And he wanted to preach to people to tell them what to do. We changed his entire speech, and he wound up getting standing ovations. One

1

client was up against four more qualified applicants for a position as executive director of a well-known lobbying group on Capitol Hill. The catch was that the new director had to be an excellent speaker. My client wasn't very good at speaking, but we worked together to improve his skills, and he got the job. My list of wonderful clients is long, I'm proud to say. They were all amazed at their transformations, and sometimes so was I.

Most of my clients actually look forward to giving presentations after we've worked together to improve their public-speaking skills. And I hope you do, too, after following the suggestions in this book. Good speechmaking.

WHAT'S IN THIS BOOK

What gives me the right to share all these pearls of wisdom with you? Experience. I've been on all sides— audience member, deliverer, and teacher.

This book fills in the gaps left by other books on writing and giving great speeches and presentations. Only someone who has given hundreds of speeches, as I have, and who has taught hundreds of clients how to write and give dynamic presentations, as I have, would know what they have left out.

The first gap has to do with the biggest mistake that many people make when they write a speech: They write for the eye, not for the ear. There is a huge difference between writing for the eye and writing for the ear. Anyone writing a speech has to know the difference before writing the first word. Most people don't.

Writing for the eye is writing an article or a letter or an editorial or a memo—something that will be read. Writing for the ear is writing something that others will hear, on television or radio or in a speech or presentation.

Some people think that whatever they write will work as a speech. Not true. In fact, I can almost guarantee that anything written for the eye will *not* be something that audiences will comprehend and retain. This book gives you the key to turning anything you've written (for the eye) into something that can be spoken and remembered.

Most books tell you to arrange the body of your speech or presentation into three points or three messages. That is one way to organize your material, but there are many other ways to consider as well. They're all here.

This book treats the question-and-answer segment of your speech differently from others. The Q&A is very important, sometimes more important than the speech itself. You should be able to answer every question authoritatively, professionally, and cordially. You don't want there to be even one question or questioner that you can't handle. This book looks at and gives solutions for every possible situation and tells you, step by step, how to handle anything that might come up.

Every book tells the reader to practice and that practice makes perfect, et cetera, et cetera. But practice means different things to different people. Some people practice by reading over the speech in their heads (which, by the way, does *nothing* to help their delivery). This book lays out for you five foolproof steps to practicing that will make you a dynamic speaker (see Chapter 5). Foolproof.

Another unique section of this book has to do with stage fright. Everyone gets it (and those who don't should go out and find some!), and every book has a chapter on it, but few tell you what you can do about it, without resorting to medication.

This book answers definitively the second most asked question about speechgiving: "What do I do with my hands?."

Those are the big ways this book is different, and they are major. In addition, the book contains dozens of valuable tips, hints, and suggestions that you've not seen elsewhere. You will learn how to avoid the ten biggest presentation no-no's:

10 NO-NO'S OF A BAD SPEECH

1. Unclear purpose or objective
2. Too much information
3. Written for the eye (to be read), not the ear (to be heard)
4. Lack of organization
5. No passion: dull writing and dull delivery
6. No gesturing
7. Not enough stories and examples (you can't have too many)
8. Not meeting the needs of the audience
9. Inappropriate dress—Looney Tunes ties and low-cut dresses are out
10. Little or no eye contact

Just reading this book will not make you a compelling, charismatic speaker, just as reading a book about tennis will not make you a great tennis player. The real learning occurs when you're on the court with the racket and the ball and, if you're lucky, a coach. Only if you put into practice what you learn here—how to write for the ear, how to practice using the five foolproof steps, how to use your hands effectively, how to recognize, accept, and handle your fear, as well as the myriad of other tips and suggestions sprinkled throughout this book—will you really learn. These are tried and true suggestions that have worked for hundreds of people.

If you hate getting up to speak in public, or you don't know how to write or give a speech, or you're just too darned scared—this book is for you.

If you've given speeches and are only okay and need fine tuning, this book is for you. If you think you're doing everything right but there seems to be something missing or you're not getting rave reviews, this book's for you.

If you've been reading your speeches to audiences and want to give them from notes, or if you have been giving speeches from notes but are ready to take the plunge to go ahead without notes—this book is for you.

PART

I

PREPARING YOUR PRESENTATION

Speeches and presentations are the most mishandled form of communication. Too often they are boring, too long, disorganized, and hard to follow. They needn't be. They shouldn't be. A good speech or presentation can enhance your image, while a bad or poorly delivered speech can damage that image and is an opportunity wasted.

A good speech is an excellent way to deliver a message. It's a chance to speak in a carefully thought out manner, to make the points *you* want, and to leave the

He can best be described as one of those orators who, before they get up, do not know what they are going to say, when they are speaking do not know what they are saying, and when they have sat down do not know what they have said.

—Winston Churchill

message *you* want to leave. It's an opportunity to sell yourself, your ideas and issues, your products and services, your company or organization, and your industry. It can give you a reputation as a thinker—someone who knows what she or he is talking about—or a doer—someone who is in action and gets things done. Being a good speaker can give you access to other audiences and opportunities. Great speakers demand and command attention.

The public-speaking teacher Dale Carnegie said that speakers need three things:

1. To have earned the right to speak on the subject.
2. To have and to convey deep feelings and convictions that put sparkle in the speaker's eyes and emotion in his or her voice; some call this passion.
3. To have many examples, stories, anecdotes, and analogies to illustrate the speaker's points and messages.

You can be an outstanding, powerful, and passionate speaker. You can impart enthusiasm, authority, and credibility. But to get there takes time and a willingness to examine your speechwriting and speechmaking and, if necessary, to put into practice new ways of writing and giving a speech.

The first step to being a great presenter is to create a presentation, which isn't as complicated as you might think. Very simply, a great presentation has these elements:

1. An opening that grabs the audience
2. A body of information that is organized in a logical, easy-to-understand manner, with many examples, analogies, anecdotes, and stories
3. Transitions—phrases that move the speech

The brain starts working the moment you're born and never stops until you get up to speak in public.

—Anonymous

along (e.g., "We've talked about the North, now let's talk about the South")

4. Short sentences
5. Easy-to-understand words
6. A stupendous closing
7. And knowing how to answer questions from the audience effectively if there is a question-and-answer segment.

Unfortunately, there is no shortcut to being a good speaker. Then again, there is no shortcut to being good at anything. Being great depends on preparation.

CHAPTER 1

INFORMATION GATHERING

SEVERAL ESSENTIAL QUESTIONS TO ASK

Before you write or speak the first word, before you do research or organize your speech, you need the answers to these key questions:

1. Whom are you talking to? Who is your audience?
2. What do you want the audience to know, do, feel or think after hearing you speak? What do you want to accomplish? What do you want your listeners to take away? What do the audience members want or need to know, or why did they invite you?

Whom Are You Talking To?

It is crucial that you know to whom you're talking. Find out as much about the audience as you possibly can (Figure 1). The more you know about your listeners, the better you'll be able to communicate with them.

You should know if your presentation must provide explanation of the issue or topic, current developments, full background on the issue, or a combination of these. Knowing your audience will affect the words you use. You will use jargon, for example, with coworkers and other industry colleagues but not with those who have little or no knowledge of your work. If Ross Perot had fully known who his audience was when he was talking to the National Association for the Advancement of Colored People (NAACP) in 1992, he never would have said, "You people. . . ."

Figure 1.   Know as much as possible about your audience.

Knowing the attitudes and the depth (or lack) of knowledge of your audience will help you organize your speech. You'll also know what demeanor to have: businesslike and professional? Suave and sophisticated? Folksy and down-to-earth?

If possible, look at the room in which your meeting will take place (Figure 2). If it is at another site, find out what you can from the meeting planner, and visit the site if possible—there may be something historical or significant about it that you can allude to in the speech. If you're short, you

Figure 2.   Be familiar with the site of your speech.

might need a box to stand on. (If so, you'll be in good company—King Hussein, Senator Barbara Mikulski, Michael Dukakis, Jack Valenti, Ted Koppel, and Queen Elizabeth all use one.) If the press will be there, don't say anything that you don't want to hear on TV or radio or see in print. There's no such thing as "off the record."

Worksheet 1: Questions to Ask the Contact When You Will Be Making a Presentation

To learn as much about your audience as possible, ask your host the following questions about your audience. Some of the information applies to in-house presentations, and some applies to presentations given to outside groups.

1. Who will be attending (with job titles), or which department(s) will be present? _____
    _____

2. How is each of the attendees connected to your topic or project? _____
    _____

3. Is the jargon in that department different from the jargon in yours? _____

4. How much time does your audience have to listen to you? _____

5. What style of presentation are they used to? (For example, some companies always use overheads.) _____

6. Name of sponsoring organization: _____
    What does it do? _____

7. Anticipated audience size: _____

8. Age (range): _____

9. Sex: _____

10. Race(s) or religion(s): _____

11. Occupation(s): _____

12. Education level(s): _____

13. National origin(s): _____

14. Socioeconomic level(s): _____

15. Interests: _____

16. How will the audience be dressed? (black tie? business attire? resort wear?):

    _____

17. Know if the audience will be supportive? friendly? neutral? hostile? _____

18. Is the audience there by choice or obligation?

    _____

19. How much does the audience know about the subject? _____

    _____

    _____

Knowing the answers to these questions before you put your presentation together can make it more relevant, understandable, and useful.

Worksheet 2: Other Questions to Ask When You Have to Give a Presentation

The answers to these questions can help you with your objective, the room setup, what comes before and after you, handouts, and other mechanics of your presentation. Ask as many questions as apply to you.

1. Why were you asked to give this presentation?

   _____

2. What are you supposed to talk about? _____

3. When is it? (date and time) _____

4. Where is the speech to be delivered (auditorium, gym, theater, restaurant, large or small meeting room)? _____

5. What is the purpose of the meeting? _____

6. What's the program or format? _____

7. What is the seating arrangement or room setup? (If you have preferences, such as round tables or seats arranged theater-style, tell the person in charge.) _____

8. How much time do you have? _____

9. Is a microphone needed? _____ If so, will it be:

    On the podium? _____

    Hand-held? _____

    Lavaliere (clip-on)? _____

    Wireless? _____

    You can request whichever you prefer.

10. What is the order of appearance (i.e., who or what precedes your presentation? Who or what follows your presentation?)? _____

11. Are you part of a panel? _____ If so, who is the moderator? (See Chapter 6.)

    _____ Phone #: _____

12. Are there other speakers? _____ If so, who are they, and what are their topics?

    _____

13. Should there be a question-and-answer segment? _____ (If one is not scheduled and you want it, request it.) How long will you have? _____

14. Will someone introduce you? _____

　　 Name: _____

　　 His/her phone number: _____

　　 Fax number: _____

15. Is it a breakfast, lunch, or dinner meeting? Will refreshments be served? _____

16. Will the press be there? _____

17. What are the travel and transportation arrangements? _____

18. What is the honorarium? _____

　　 Will the check be there, or should you send a bill?

　　 _____

19. If you have handouts, how many copies will you need? _____

　　 When should they be at the meeting site? _____

　　 _____

20. Are arrangements being made for your spouse or other person who is accompanying you? _____

21. What equipment will you need (i.e., slide projector, VCR, overhead)? (Also put your request in writing.) _____

22. Do you need a box to stand on so that everyone can see you while you're speaking? _____

> A talk is a voyage with a purpose, and it must be charted. The person who starts out going nowhere, generally gets there.
>
> —Dale Carnegie

The Objective: What You Want the Audience to Know

The objective is the reason you are giving the presentation. It is either:

a. What you want the audience to know, think, feel, or remember, or

b. What the audience wants to know—the reason you were invited, or

c. A combination of the two. Do you want it to know that sales were down for this past quarter? Do you want it to feel proud to be a donor to your non-profit? Do you want it to think that there might be some truth to the sexual harassment accusations made by some people of your office? Do you want it to sign a petition or vote a certain way?

Your objective is your destination. If you don't understand where you're going, the audience certainly won't. If you're not clear about what you want the audience to know, and you can't say or write it in a relatively short sentence, there is no way the audience will understand you.

Knowing your objective is crucial. It provides a clear sense of direction and, if you let it, helps you stay focused and eliminate superfluous information. It tells you (and the audience) where you're going.

To write your objective, finish this sentence: "When I'm through speaking, I want my audience to _____

Here are some examples of effective objectives:

Know that we are worthy of a donation because we have a vision and goals, are well-organized, and are getting the job done. (Objective of a speech by the director of a nonprofit to an audience of people connected to foundations that make contributions to non-profits.)

Know what's going on in Washington that affects their industry. (Objective of a Washington lobbyist speaking to members of a trade association at their annual meeting.)

Know how our department will reach its goals in the next year. (Objective of department head to top management in a large company.)

Once you have a clear objective, every sentence or paragraph must relate to it. It's the only way the audience can follow you and get your message.

RESEARCH

Don't ever agree to give a speech on a subject you know little or nothing about, no matter how much you will be paid or what you think you'll get out of it. If you're not an expert, you'll never be able to do enough research to appear to be one. And if you could do a great deal of research, you'd never be comfortable enough with the subject to give the speech with the air of authority and credibility that real experts have. Better to stick to your area(s) of expertise.

Sometimes, though, even experts need to do research. If this is the case, learn everything you can about the subject of the speech, far more than you'll ever use. Review all the files related to your project or topic. If possible, talk to employees who are directly involved with your topic or project. Get into your subject. Get the subject into you. It's the only way you have a chance of getting the subject into your audience. Go to the Internet, Prodigy, AmericaOnline, CompuServe; use computerized databases like Nexus and Lexis; visit university and association libraries; write to trade associations; read books, pamphlets, other speeches, and newspaper and magazine articles about your topic, and talk to experts. Often, the more you know, the more excited and passionate you'll be. And the more you can show that excitement and passion, the greater your chance of connecting with your audience and making an impact.

A computer expert who knew everything about computers and trends and microprocessors was invited to speak to a state education association about computers in the classroom. He knew generally about computers in classrooms but not what was going on in that state. No matter, he thought. He would dust off the computer speech he'd given to a large company the month before.

After visiting a speech coach he thought better of that plan and started to research computers in the classroom. He called computer companies and the National Education Association, and amassed printed material and computer programs for students. He was a hit and was subsequently invited to other state education associations. Now he is singlehandedly having an impact on computer use in classrooms in the United States.

If you're going to be giving several speeches on the same or related topics, start a file with ideas, interesting stories, quotations, jokes, bits of information, and power words. Those you can't use this time may fit into a future presentation. Voltaire always carried a scribbling book and jotted down thoughts and ideas to include in his orations.

Worksheet 3: Create Your Own Scribbling Book

Is there a story you've told that has always worked? Write it here so that you don't forget it.

_____

_____

_____

Did you hear an interesting story, joke, remark, or quote recently that you forgot to write down?
Write it here. _____

_____

_____

_____

After doing your research, look at your material with an eye toward organizing it in a way that an audience can follow.

CHAPTER 2

OUTLINING YOUR PRESENTATION

After you have completed your research, the next step in preparing your presentation is to put together an outline or plan. During this phase you plan the basic structure and contents of your talk and consider which presentation styles you will use to give your presentation. This is not, however, the time to plan the actual words that you will use—that comes later.

Speeches are given to:

- *Persuade,* which includes *inspire, sell, convince,* and get the audience to *do, know,* or *think* what you want it to.
- *Inform,* which includes *educate, commemorate,* and *enlighten.*
- *Entertain* (*entre*-between + *tenir*-to hold), to *hold the attention of, interest, amuse.* Make no mistake; your speech is a performance. You have to hold your audience's interest throughout.

Your information must be organized in a way that is easy for your audience to follow. If you get up there and say whatever comes into your mind, the audience will be totally confused and come away with nothing.

METHODS OF ORGANIZATION

There are many ways to organize your material. You should select the method that best suits your objective and the information you want to impart. The first three methods described in this section are the most widely used.

Chronological or Sequential Order

When you use a chronological order, you describe what happened first, second, third, and so on. You order your remarks in terms of Past-Present-Future—where we were, where we are, and where we're going. A variation of this order is, Present-Past-Future, describes where we are, where we were or how we got here, and where we're going. This is a very effective order for nonprofits to use in fund-raising:

Present: *Sarah's Circle, a home for low-income elderly, provides. . . .*

Past: *But it wasn't always that way. In 1980, . . .*

Future: *But all this isn't enough. To take care of the needs of the elderly poor, Sarah's Circle still needs. . . .*

Three-Point Technique

One of the easiest ways to organize your presentation is to figure out three points or messages you want to convey or group your information into three areas. Audiences can take in three points but not much more. The three areas the computer journalist discussed with the state education association were:

1. Computer technology yesterday, today, and tomorrow, including trends
2. Where schools are today in computer use
3. What it will take to get more computers into classrooms

A hospital administrator might want to talk about

1. *Care*—The care the patients receive
2. *Research*—The research done at the hospital that has led to breakthroughs
3. *Education*—What it means to be a teaching hospital

Problem-Cause-Solution Technique

If there is a problem or if you want to persuade, convince, inspire, or motivate the audience (not) to do something, you need to lay out the problem(s), give its cause and consequences or the evidence for your view, and conclude with a solution, which is often a call to action and describes what you want the audience to do. You must know the audience's stand and your stand on this issue or problem before you use this formula.

Problem: Youth and drugs
Cause: Society and lack of parental supervision
Solution: Drug rehab agency and parent education

Problem: Welfare
Cause: Current program makes people dependent on a system; started as a temporary stopgap measure and lasted 60 years
Solution: Welfare reform that includes job training and day care

Inductive Reasoning Technique

The inductive reasoning approach uses logic to appeal to people. A progression of facts and their connections lead to the desired conclusion. For example:

Fact: Homelessness is increasing in this city.
Fact: Homeless people need help.
Fact: Homelessness can be turned around.
Fact: Our agency helps homeless people.
Conclusion: With our help, we can get people shelter (therefore, please donate money to our organization).

Contrast-and-Compare Technique

This simple approach points out the similarities and differences between two issues, events or groups, such as Republicans and Democrats, 1956 and 1996, or slavery and the Holocaust.

Numerical Technique

Using this method of organization in a presentation requires that you break your information into items that can be listed: Five things to know about starting a new company, three things to know before getting married; seven reasons to reorganize our company.

Alphabetical Technique

In a presentation to an audience that wanted to be entertained and taught how to make speeches, one woman used the letters in word PRESENTATION to get her message across:

> P — Practice
> R — Read your audience
> E — Ear, not eye
> S — Short words, short sentences
> E — Examples
> N — Never be boring
> T — Transitions
> A — Answers and questions
> T — Time
> I — Introductions
> O — Openings and closings
> N — Nervous, stage fright

"OREO" Technique

The "OREO" Technique uses research and example to back up an opinion, which frames the presentation:
Opinion: *There should be a rating system for TV shows in an attempt to cut down on the violence that children see on television.*
Research: *Studies show that there is a relationship between what young people see on TV (and in the movies) and what they do out on the street.*

Example(s): *Give stories, details, illustrations, or anecdotal evidence that supports your research.*

Opinion: *There should be a rating system for TV shows in an attempt to cut down on violence that children see on television.*

STORIES

After you decide how you will organize your presentation, you need to select stories, examples, anecdotes, or analogies to illustrate your important points. You can never tell too many. Audiences love stories and will remember them longer than they will remember anything else about your talk.

The audience will feel more friendly toward you if you share something personal. You can be controversial, but not insulting. Generally, tell stories about topics with which the audience might be familiar. A story about farming will probably have more impact on farmers or other ag-related businesspeople than on accountants from the city. Avoid dialects and accents unless you are good at them and your story is not putting anyone down. Don't tell a story you haven't practiced or do not know well.

First Lady Hillary Rodham Clinton's objective for most of her speaking engagements during the time she was being questioned about her role in the Whitewater land scandal was to do or say whatever it took to get the audiences to like and support her (more). In 1996, at a Valentine's Day book party in Washington, D.C., attended by five hundred women, she reused a story she had told a week before to one thousand women at the annual meeting of the Association of Junior Leagues International.

Years before Bill Clinton became president, he, Mrs. Clinton, and Chelsea, then five years old, were in church in Little Rock, Arkansas, on Valentine's Day. There were several children at the altar, including Chelsea, and the minister asked them what they would give their mothers for Valentine's Day if they could give them anything. One little boy said, "The biggest bunch of flowers he could find." A little girl said, "A dress made of diamonds." Chelsea Clinton said, "Life insurance" (which got a laugh). Hillary said she was somewhat embarrassed at the time, especially when all the insurance salesmen in the church later approached her (this got a laugh, too). On the way home, she asked Chelsea why she had said that. The child replied, "Because I want you to live forever, Mommy" (which brought yet another reaction from the audience).

Hillary Clinton told the following story on herself at least a dozen times after the release of her book, *It Takes a Village and Other Lessons Children Teach Us,* but only to audiences of women.

> *Right after Chelsea was born, I was breast-feeding her when she started foaming at the nose* [always got a laugh]. *I was afraid Chelsea was having convulsions so I buzzed the nurses who came running in. I beseeched the nurses, pointing to Chelsea. They told me it would help if I would lift Chelsea's head up* [always got a laugh]. *I felt so stupid. I knew I needed help. I needed the help of a village.*

She related it the same way on both occasions—same pauses, same beseeching tones—and she got the same laughs. She aimed it at the right audience—women, many of whom could identify with her. The story made her one of them, and it was humorous. Of course, she also neatly worked in the title of her book.

Many of your stories can be told over and over, depending on your delivery and your audience. Chances are usually slim to none that someone will have heard it before, and if someone has, so be it. But every time you tell stories, you have to show the enthusiasm and interest you showed the first time.

Start sentences with "Picture this," and use vivid language that puts pictures in people's minds to describe what you're talking about.

In 1988 the Democratic presidential candidate, Michael Dukakis, wanted to talk about medical insurance being a shambles. To illustrate, he told the story of a little boy who couldn't participate in sports because his father couldn't afford medical insurance. Evoking that little boy sitting on the sidelines watching his friends play when he couldn't is a lot more moving than stating that the medical insurance industry is a mess.

Your objective is your destination. An outline is how you are going to get there—the route you will take that is logical and easy to follow for your audience. Worksheet 3 is an outline that works, and you may want to make copies of it for future speeches or presentations.

Write a "25-word-or-fewer" sentence that explains what your speech is about. This is your objective, i.e., what you want the audience to know or do after your speech. Every part of your speech should relate to your objectives. If *you're* not clear what your objective is, your audience never will be.

Outline for Writing a Speech

Open

Transition

1. Point

    Example(s)

Transition

2. Point

    Example(s)

Transition

3. Point

   Example(s)

Transition: "I've given you a lot of information—I want to hear what's on your mind. . . ."

Question-and-Answer Segment

Transition

Close.

Worksheet 4: Your Presentation Outline

What is your objective? _____

_____

_____

_____

Which type of organization works best for your material? (Circle one)

    Past-Present-Future

    Present-Past-Future

    Three Points

    Problem-Cause-Solution

    Inductive Reasoning

    Contrast-and-Compare

    Numerical

    Alphabetical

    "OREO"

How will you illustrate each point with stories, anecdotes, examples, details, and analogies?

Point 1: (Problem: past, present) _____

_____

_____

Stories/examples: _____

_____

_____

Point 2: (Cause: present, past) _____

_____

Stories/examples: _____

_____

_____

Point 3: (Solution: future) _____

_____

_____

Stories/examples: _____

_____

_____

Types of Openers

There are many ways to open your presentation. Some possibilities include:

• *Provide a preview of what your speech is about.* This is the first part of that old saying, "Tell 'em what you're going to tell 'em. Tell 'em. Tell 'em what you told 'em."

Everyone wants us to pick it up, but no one wants us to put it down.—former New Jersey Governor James Florio on toxic waste disposal.

• Describe a personal experience or tell a human interest story. Paint a picture, give a dramatic illustration, or tell any story that is relevant. Remember, audiences love stories.

My best marketing success story? How I put a personal ad in a magazine and met my wife.

Did you know that Emma Glotz was scared to death to walk out of her house at night? Now, she walks a mile every night. Why? Operation Safestreet, that's why.

• *Ask a question.* This involves the audience. For example:

A television news director asked an audience, *How many of you will watch the 6 P.M. news tonight to see a murder in another city?* No hands went up. Then he asked, *How many of you will watch the 6 P.M. news tonight to see a murder that happened a mile from your house?* All hands went up. He had them.

An anesthesiologist asked an audience how many members would be concerned about the pain of an operation or the recovery period. All hands went up, and the audience wanted to hear more.

A minister asked an unsuspecting audience, *How many of you have read the Bible?*

A nice-looking man in a business suit asked, *Do I look like a prison warden?*

• *Ask a rhetorical question.* Another way to engage the audience, but this one isn't looking for a response from it.

"Who am I, and why am I here?" Vice Admiral James Stockdale (ret.), H. Ross Perot's 1992 vice presidential running mate

Do you eat to live or live to eat?

When will the American taxpayer put his/her foot down and say, "No more"?

• *Pose a hypothetical situation.* Get your audience to imagine a scenario that you describe. Start with phrases like, *What if* or *Let's pretend for a moment.*

• *Describe something new or dramatic in your industry or area of expertise*—natural gas-powered cars, diet pills that work, a medical or computer breakthrough, the results of a new study.

• *Make a startling statement, fact, or statistic* that attracts attention, arouses curiosity, surprises the audience, or is particularly informative. For example:

The average person spends about 220,000 hours asleep during his or her lifetime.

The average mother who holds a job outside the home works an eighty-four-hour week to meet her responsibilities at work and at home.

There are 250 million people in the United States. There are 200 million handguns.

• *Compliment the audience or the introducer or someone at the presentation.* If you do this sincerely, you come off looking very gracious. This opening is often used by politicians with audiences that helped them get elected or get a law or regulation passed, by executive directors of nonprofits with donors, and by presidents of successful companies to employees. Here's an example:

Thank you very much for that warm welcome, and thank you, Patricia, for those very kind words of introduction and for this beautiful award. And I must say that if there was a best-seller list at the Red Cross, Patricia Aburdene's *Megatrends for Women* would be right on top. I frequently see the book on the desk of some of our top managers, and I have quoted from your book quite often in recent speeches. Thank you for such a wealth of information and creative ideas!

—Elizabeth Dole

* *Identify with the audience.*

It's great to be back in [name of city]. *This building was my grade school forty years ago.*

Like you, I'm a salesperson. Everyone is a salesperson.

* *Use a significant or familiar quotation.* Quotations can be effective, but never say "quote unquote" or use more than two or three quotations in any speech.

Whatever you can do or dream you can, begin it. Boldness has genius, power, and magic in it.—Johann Wolfgang von Goethe (1749–1832)

The return from your work must be the satisfaction which that work brings you and the world's need of that work. With this, life is heaven, or as near to heaven as you can get. Without this—with work which you despise, which bores you, and which the world does not need—this life is hell.—W. E. B. DuBois

Politics is the art of looking for trouble, finding it everywhere, diagnosing it incorrectly, and applying the wrong remedies—Groucho Marx

* *Mention something related to the headlines or recent news.* This suggestion applies to events no more than three or four months in the past. Republicans, Bosnia, cults, politics, congressional battles, welfare reform, and AIDS were all topical in 1996; the 1991 Persian Gulf War was not.

I want to talk about something that's broken—namely our civil justice system—and about some way to fix it. Voltaire once said of the Holy Roman Empire that it was neither holy, nor Roman, nor an empire. The same

*might be said of the civil justice system in the United
States—it is neither civil, nor just, nor a system.*
—Stephen Middlebrook, Aetna Life & Casualty

Humor

Once upon a time, a lion was wandering through a forest
and spied a bull. He got very close, undetected, and pounced
on the bull. After a tussle, the lion killed the bull and had a
fabulous feast for a week. After his last bite, he licked his
lips, and settled in for a long, deep sleep. When the lion
awoke, he stretched slowly and was so proud of himself that
he roared and roared. A hunter heard him, followed the
sound until he found him, centered him in the site of his
gun, and killed him with one shot. The moral of the story?
When you are full of bull, keep your mouth shut! (Figure
3.) This story is from a person who teaches people how to
speak and talk to the media.

A common tip given in many speechmaking books is always
to start with a joke or a funny story. (Figure 4.) DON'T
unless:

- You're naturally funny.
- You are certain you can deliver the joke or story hu-
  morously to this particular audience.
- The joke or story is appropriate and/or relevant.

Figure 3.   Keep your mouth shut when you're full of
"bull."

Figure 4. Don't use jokes unless they're relevant and you can tell them in a humorous way.

Don't use ethnic or off-color jokes. Keep your jokes clean, nondiscriminating, and kind. Don't use self-deprecating humor or humor that belittles your competence (people in the audience will subconsciously wonder why they're listening to you). Don't use humor that belittles someone else's competence (à la Don Rickles).

Poking fun at yourself is the safest kind of humor.

> *I haven't seen this much interest in me since the grand jury.*—Hillary Clinton to one thousand women at a book party for her book, *It Takes a Village.*

> *I'm going to speak my mind because I have nothing to lose.*—S. I. Hayakawa

If you are funny, keep a notebook of (clean) humorous stories you've heard or read to be used at the appropriate time. If another person on the program with you is funny, too, let him/her shine. Don't cut into his/her humor or feel defensive or act as if you're in a contest. Most audiences will be glad to have two funny speakers instead of one. Enjoy each other.

If you are not funny, don't even think about using humor.

OPENING

The opening of your presentation is crucial. (Figure 5.) It sets the tone for the whole presentation. How you deliver your opening can mean the difference between success and failure, between being likable and having the audience want to listen to you and turning them off.

There's no rule that says you have to start with "good afternoon" or "It's a pleasure to be here" or even "Thank you." You can use these openers, but you can also be creative. Many speakers just jump right into their openings. Even though he's not making a speech or presentation per se, Ted Koppel on ABC's *Nightline* jumps right into his subject every night.

Your opening has to be brilliant and strong and attention-getting. You want to grab your audience, cause a reaction in it—good or bad, positive or negative. Consider how this opening would make audience members perk up their ears.

> *Senior citizens should be put in homes and ignored,* said former Colorado Governor Richard Lamm. Even though he didn't mean exactly that, the audience reacted strongly and wanted to hear more.
>
> *Repricing stinks.* Said by the last speaker, a community activist, several years ago at a hearing at the

Figure 5.   Your opening must be brilliant.

Council on Wage and Price Stability. It was the only sound bite picked up by the network news the whole day.

As Henry VIII said to each of his wives, I won't keep you long.

I appreciate your welcome. And as the cow said to the Maine farmer, "Thank you for a warm hand on a cold morning."—John F. Kennedy on the campaign trail.

You have only thirty seconds to two minutes to capture the audience's attention. The audience makes up its mind about you in that short time period, so you want it engaged from the very first moments.

Worksheet 5: Draft Your Opener

Go back and look at all the suggested ways to open a speech. Think of something that will evoke a response—positive or negative—from the audience of your next speech. Write it here._____

_____

_____

_____

_____

> **A speech is like a love affair; any fool can start one but to end it requires considerable skill.**
>
> —Lord Mancraft (1914-1987)

CLOSING

Unfortunately, most people don't have the considerable skill needed to close. Many don't even think about the closing. They get to the end of what they want to say, say thank you, and sit down.

The closing is your last chance to leave the audience with a positive image of you, your topic or project, your department or workteam, your company or organization, and your industry. It's your final chance to tell the people in the audience what you want them to know or do when you're finished talking. It will be the last thing the audience hears and may be the only thing the audience remembers. It must therefore be outstanding and remarkable.

The best closings are direct, brief, and strong. *Do not wing it.* It's too important.

If there's something in particular that you'd like your audience to remember, try using this phrase, "If you take away only one thing from this speech, ..."

Closing Styles

As with the opening, there is no one way to close. Here are a number of possibilities (the first three closings are used most often):

• *Issue a call to action.* If you want the audience to do, think, feel, know, or say something, say so. Don't be vague or obtuse. If you want it to use your services or department, vote a certain way, write letters, put more computers in classrooms, donate organs after death—be direct: "Let me urge you to . . . ." If sales are down and you want them up, say so, and give the audience some how-to's. If you want them to think differently about people of color, say, "The next time you see an African-American hailing a cab. . . ."

• *Provide a summary.* Stress or review your main points, or refer to or repeat parts of your opening. Tell 'em what you just told 'em: "Let me review. . . ." The audience usually can't go back and reread your speech, so a summary always works as a closing.

• *Predict the future.* "By the year 2000 or 2010, we will barely recognize the computers we are using today. That's why it's important that we . . ."; "Our sales are X million. I predict by the year 2005, our sales will have doubled."

• *Challenge the audience.* Give it a goal to work toward. "I challenge you to double your sales by the end of the year"; "I challenge you parents to play a part in your children's education by becoming more involved in their schools"; "I challenge our entire industry to clean up its act. I can tell you that our firm, the XVY Company, will be a role model for those who share our vision."

• *Remind the audience of a stirring statement.* President John F. Kennedy's peroration in his 1961 inaugural address is most often used: "Ask not what your country can do for you; ask what you can do for your country." Many other moving words by a variety of authors can be found in any book of quotations.

"Man is born to live and not to prepare to live."— Boris Pasternak

"Discovery consists of what everybody has seen and thinking what nobody has thought."—Albert Szent-Gyorgyi

• *Tell an anecdote or story.* Use an anecdote to illustrate your main point.

A young monk entered a monastery where the monks were only allowed to speak two words every ten years. After ten years, he was asked how things were going. "Bed hard," he said. Ten years later he was asked the same question. "Room cold," he said. At the end of thirty years, he was asked the same question. "I quit," he said. "Good riddance," he was told. "You've been crabbing ever since you got here!" The message is that it doesn't take much to leave a negative impression.

• *Ask a rhetorical question. So which will it be? Higher taxes or less education for our kids?* Sometimes you'll answer the question, and sometimes you'll leave the audience hanging. If your opening was a rhetorical question, you can use the same one for your closing. For example, *So I ask again, When will the American taxpayer put his or her foot down and say, "No more"?*

• *Offer a bit of advice.* This can be a bit tricky, so be careful. Most people don't like to be told what to do, especially when it has to do with judgment. (They like to think they thought of the solution, whatever it is.) But there are exceptions. If you're a stockbroker telling people what stocks to buy, the audience can't write fast enough. If you're an educator or a child psychologist telling parents that they should spend more time with their children, be careful.

• *Make a pledge or promise.* Candidates and presidents of corporations love to use this; but be careful. Don't promise anything you can't do or cause to happen. People remember the darndest things, and if your promise is captured on audio- or videotape, especially if you don't keep your word, it will come back to haunt you.

• *Try a bit of humor, but only if you're funny.* The same rule applies here as in our discussion of openings: Use humor *only if you can pull it off* (Figure 4).

Watch the Clock

You have one to two minutes at the most for your closing. Once you say, "Finally" or "In conclusion," the clock is ticking. You don't want to be one of those speakers who cue the audience that the end is near but is still speaking twenty minutes later. (Even worse are those speakers who say, "Before I close" and then speak for another twenty minutes before they even begin to close!)

Always cue the audience that the end is near: "In conclusion. . . ." Memorize your closing or know it well enough so that you can have total eye contact. You need a lot of energy and passion to end with a bang, so don't let your energy or voice fade away as you conclude.

If it's appropriate, let the audience know of other meetings and seminars and books on the subject of your talk.

What orators lack in depth, they make up to you in length.

—Charles de Montesquieu (1689–1755)

Worksheet 6: Draft Your Closing

Think back to or look back at your last speech. What did your closing say? Was it as effective as it could have been? What would have made it more effective?

_____

_____

Write a closing that would have been more effective.

_____

_____

_____

_____

_____

Think of your next speech. What conclusion will work for that audience?_____

_____

_____

_____

Now again, use the following to put your next speech or presentation together. You know your opening, the points you want to make, some or all of your examples, and the closing. You still need the transitions, and you may need more examples, but you can come back and fill them in later. Make copies of this outline to help you with future speeches or presentations.

Repetition is the mother of skill.

—Dr. John DeLuca

Outline for Writing a Speech

Open

Transition

1. Point

  Example(s)

Transition

2. Point

  Example(s)

Transition

3. Point

  Example(s)

Transition: "I've given you a lot of information—I want to hear what's on your mind. . . ."

Question-and-Answer Segment

Transition

Close

Worksheet 7: Outline for Writing a Speech

Objective: Write here a 25-word-or-less sentence that explains what you want the audience to know or do, after your speech. (If *you're* not clear what your objective is, your audience never will be.):

_____

_____

_____

_____

_____

Opening: (2–3 minutes, 1 page, typed, double spaced):

_____

_____

_____

_____

_____

_____

_____

_____

_____

_____

_____

_____

_____

_____

_____

_____

_____

Transition:_____

_____

_____

Body: (14–16 minutes, 6 pages) Use the following lines to note your main points, examples or anecdotes, and transitions. When you write the body of your presentation, attach it to this outline.

Point 1:_____

_____

_____

_____

Stories/examples:_____

_____

_____

_____

_____

_____

_____

_____

Transition:_____

_____

Point 2:_____

_____

_____

_____

Stories/examples:_____

_____

_____

_____
_____
_____
_____
_____

Transition:_____
_____

Point 3:_____
_____
_____
_____
_____

Stories/examples:_____
_____
_____
_____
_____
_____
_____

Transition to Q&A:_____
_____

Question-and-answer segment: (10–15 minutes)

Transition to Closing:_____
_____
_____

Closing: 1½–2 minutes, ½ page–1 page, typed and double spaced)

In conclusion, _____

_____

_____

_____

_____

_____

_____

_____

_____

_____

_____

_____

_____

_____

_____

_____

_____

_____

_____

_____

Now you're almost ready to write out your speech word for word.

CHAPTER 3

PUTTING IT INTO WORDS

You're clear about your objective, you've done any research that needs to be done, you've found the way to organize your material that makes it easy for the audience to understand, you've thought up and collected several ways to illustrate the (three) points you want to make, and you're working on both your opening and your closing. Now it's almost time to start writing your presentation. (See Figure 6.)

WRITE FOR THE EAR

Before you write out your presentation word for word, with sentences and paragraphs, it's essential that you take care to avoid the biggest mistake that people make at this point. When you write from your head to your hand to your computer screen (or head to hand to paper), your words (usually)

Figure 6.   Write for the ear, not for the eye.

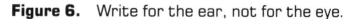

come out for the eye, that is, as something to be read (Figure 7). You probably have used long sentences and big words, and the result is more like an article or a letter or a memo than a speech.

There's a big difference between writing for the eye and writing for the ear. You can't write a great or even a good speech until you know what that difference is.

When something is written for the eye—to be read—readers who don't understand a word, a phrase, or a sentence, can go back and read it again and again until they do understand it. Writing for the ear—that is, writing a speech or presentation—is totally different. Listeners have only one chance to understand what the speaker is saying. They're not going to tape the presentation and play it back, and they're not going to raise their hands every time a speaker says a word or phrase they don't understand to ask for clarification.

When you're writing for the ear, your sentences have to be short—a maximum of twenty words—and the words have to be easily understood.

Writing for the ear is tricky. There are two ways to do this: Either talk as you write—that is, from your head to your mouth to your fingertips to the computer screen—or, after the piece is written, read it aloud, shortening sentences to no more than twenty words. You will make your presentation conversational by simplifying words and shortening sentences.

Crafting sentences that contain twenty words or fewer is key. Each sentence should have only one thought in it, because that is all listeners can understand (longer sentences have two and three thoughts, which can be confusing). Shorter sentences have the added benefit of being much easier to deliver than longer ones. We talk in sentences that have twenty words or fewer. It's a conversational length, which means you won't run out of breath, as you would reading a sentence with thirty-five or forty-three words or

> **I notice that you use plain, simple language, short words, and brief sentences. That is the way to write English—it is the modern way and the best way. Stick to it, and don't let fluff and flowers and verbosity creep in.**
>
> **—Mark Twain (to a twelve-year-old boy).**

Figure 7. Top: Mouth to head to hands to computer screen (or paper) comes out written for the ear. Bottom: Head to hands to computer screen (or paper) comes out written for the eye.

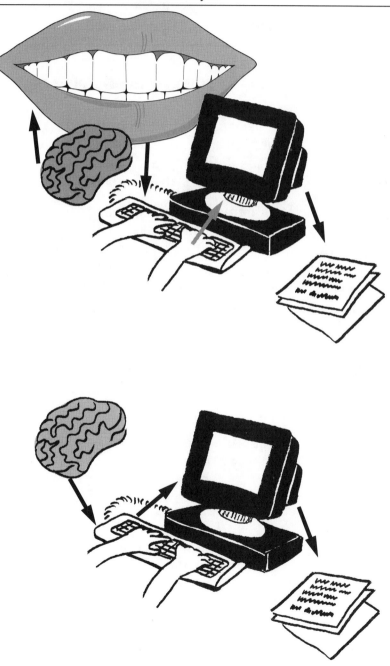

more! Short sentences are often stronger than long ones, anyway.

Your goal is to educate your listeners by talking with them, not by preaching, teaching, orating, or pontificating. You want to communicate effectively with your audience, not impress them.

Worksheet 8: Writing Exercise

Here's a sentence from *The Washington Post* that was, of course, written for the eye. See if you can rewrite it for the ear. Write it as if you were talking to your neighbor over the back fence.

Example: An unexpected surge in employment last month paradoxically sent the stock and bond markets into a tailspin yesterday, as traders pushed aside the good news and focused instead on the likelihood that a stronger economy could mean higher interest rates.

You rewrite: _____

_____

_____

_____

_____

Possible answer, written for the ear:
There was an unexpected rise in employment last month, which caused stock and bond prices to fall. Experts say the higher employment figures could mean higher interest rates.

Explanation. In conversation, we don't start sentences with clauses, and most of us don't typically use six-syllable words (paradoxically). A forty-word sentence has too many thoughts in it for listeners to follow it easily, and you would have to take several breaths delivering it. The word *traders* could also be heard as *traitors* which would be confusing.

Analogies

Analogies serve multiple purposes in writing. In addition to illustrating a point, they can be used to make a point.

> For every aluminum can you recycle, you save enough energy to operate your television set for three hours.

You can use as many analogies as you want. Some analogies have a "gee whiz" factor; people often say, "Gee whiz, I didn't know that" after hearing them. For example, one in a million is the same as one second out of 11½ days; one in a billion is equivalent to one second out of 31½ years. Or consider this: If you had received a trillion dollars on the day Jesus was born and spent a million dollars a day every day since, you would not run out of money until August 2739!

Whether an analogy is good or not depends on your audience. Try one out and see how an audience reacts. If it reacts in some way, you've got a good one. Here are some effective analogies:

> To describe a Wal-Mart Hypermart: *Harold Young recently roamed through the 225,000-square-foot store—as big as five football fields—looking for Canada Dry Club Soda. He couldn't find it.—Business Week*

> *Some whites are to people of color like causing a storm, then passing out umbrellas and expecting us to say thanks.*—Rev. Al Sharpton

> *The savings and loan crisis is like rearranging the chairs on the Titanic.*

> *What you have here is an administration that set its hair on fire and is trying to put it out with a hammer.*—New York Senator Al D'Amato on the failed attempt to oust the Panamanian dictator Manuel Noriega in 1988

Being a member of the United Way is like being on a football team in that we have to work together to succeed.

WRITING YOUR SPEECH

Now it's time to write your speech out, word for word, in full sentences, with paragraphs, an opening, transitions, a body, and a closing. It's time to turn your outline into text. You'll need eight to ten pages of text that is typed double spaced for a twenty-minute presentation.

Someone asked Ernest Hemingway many years ago how to write a novel. He is reported to have said, "First you clean out the refrigerator." For many, writing is a daunting, often lonely task. If you're a normal human being, you will put off writing your speech and then put it off some more. The way to "just do it" is to give up correct typing, correct spelling, and correct punctuation for the moment and, using your outline as a guide, just write, mistakes and all. Know that you will not write the perfect speech when you sit down and write the first draft. In fact, there may be little relationship between your first draft and what you end up delivering. Even the greatest speechwriters will tell you that writing a great speech is an evolutionary process.

There are several ways to write your speech. You can write the opening and the closing first, then the body; you can write the body, then add the opening and closing; or you can start at the opening and go to the end. Trial lawyers write the end first and work backwards. Most people prefer to write the body first, then the opening and closing. Do whatever works.

Again, write a "25-word-or-fewer" sentence that explains what your speech is about. This is your objective, i.e., what you want the audience to know or do after your speech. Every part of your speech should relate to your objective. If *you're* not clear what your objective is, your audience never will be.

> **I do think people can become better and worthier if they are ambitious about speaking well, and they are enamored with being able to persuade their hearers.**
>
> **—Isocrates, Athenian orator (436–338 B.c)**

It's important to write out your entire speech, even though you will not read it but will deliver it from notes (or preferably without any papers at all, but more on that later). Your paragraphs should have three to five sentences. If they're any shorter, they may be undeveloped; if they're too much longer, they may be too complex. You want to make sure your sentences aren't too long and that everything fits together nicely. Remember, sentences should be no more than twenty words in length. You also want to make sure you've included all your points and in the right order and that the length is within the time frame.

Flesh out the examples, stories, illustrations, and details as you're writing. Don't forget to talk them as you write them, making sure you're using words that put pictures in people's minds. The examples are often more important than the point you're making.

You will need a written-out speech to practice, to hand to a last-minute replacement in case you can't make it, and maybe to distribute as a handout and to give to the press.

Every sentence in the speech should relate to your objective and have relevance for the audience. Any information in your speech that doesn't have relevance for the audience or meet its needs should be deleted.

As you write or proofread every sentence, ask yourself: Does it relate to my objective? Does it excite? Does it amuse? Does it clarify what I'm saying? Can my listeners relate to it? If any answer is no, go back and edit.

Words

Use words that are simple, familiar, and easy to understand. Use the "nickel" word, even if you think the "dollar" one is more impressive.

> FDR said, *We are endeavoring to construct a more inclusive society.* He could have said, *We're going to make a country in which no one is left out.*

If you use a long, difficult word, the audience will miss the next ten words figuring out what you said. Keep it simple. Remember, you're writing for the ear, not for the eye.

> *By hard, honest labor, I've dug all the large words out of my vocabulary. I never write "metropolis" for seven cents because I can get "city" for the same price. I never write "policeman" because I can get "cop" for the same price.—Mark Twain*

> *In choosing words remember when you write and speak, That little words are often strong and long ones often weak.—Charles Osgood*

Winston Churchill, an eloquent and erudite orator, often used one-syllable words: *Give us the tools and we will do the job.*

Use words and terms that are easy to envision and that can be related to familiar things. What if you heard someone speak about something that measures 47,000 square feet? Would you be able to imagine how big that is? Is it the size of your living room? The lobby of the Hotel Anatole in Dallas or the Opryland Hotel in Nashville? If the speaker had said instead that the space was the size of a football field, wouldn't you have been able to picture it immediately? When you say something measures 47,000 square feet without explaining it, the audience misses the next ten words or so trying to figure out how big 47,000 square feet is. If you use words that put pictures in people's minds, the audience can follow your presentation more easily.

Here's another example of the same thing. Consider the phrase "one part per billion." It sounds small, but how small? If someone says it's the equivalent of one drop of water in a bathtub, you can picture it.

Important Do's and Don'ts

Even though you are on the right road, with a clear objective, have chosen an organization that is easy for the audience to follow, are keeping your sentences to twenty words, there are still some do's and don'ts that make your speech more dynamic.

The Do's

- *Use plays on words.*

I challenge anyone to look around the room this evening . . . and to tell us why the ''glass ceiling'' shouldn't meet the same fate as the Berlin Wall.—Elizabeth Dole to the National Foundation of Women Business Owners

- *Use groups of three. This can be very effective.*

A convention speaker once remarked: *There are three things I have never wanted to be: the front pew in a church, the sixth verse of a hymn, and the last speaker on a convention program.*

People can be divided into three groups: those who make things happen, those who watch things happen, and those who wonder what happened.

Reaching the top lay leadership position at XXX after twenty years of service fills me with pride, excitement, and humility: pride in the recognition and confidence being accorded me by my peers; excitement for the great challenges that lie ahead, and humility in the face of the great leaders who have come before me.

You can also use the same phrase three times:

So they believe as we believe that unions are indispensable to the quality of our lives.
So they believe as we believe that only through unions can workers truly redress their grievances.
So they believe as we believe that only through unions can workers have a respected voice in the workplace . . .

and have security with their jobs . . . and security in their retirement.

• *Use words that affect the senses of touch, smell, sight, sound, and taste.* If you hear a phrase such as "He looked as if he were sucking a lemon wedge," you can picture him. These are also evocative: "It felt like velvet"; "It smelled like rotten eggs."

• *Steal a good line from someone:* Walter Mondale stole a line from a Wendy's commercial when he asked Gary Hart "Where's the beef?" Many speakers have quoted President Ronald Reagan, who "had it up to his keester" (wherever on the anatomy that is!) and President George Bush, who said on more than one occasion, "We're in deep doo-doo."

• *Be clever.* Massachusetts Representative Ed Markey paraphrased Shakespeare when he said about the stealth bomber, "B-2 or not B-2, that is the question."

• *Offer the unexpected.* Try "Least but certainly not last" or "and her lovely husband."

• *Include the phrase "What this means to you is. . . ."* Try this if you want to persuade the audience to do or not to do something or to sell them something, be it a product or an idea. These words wake up those who have tuned out and make them sit up and listen.

• *If you are going to inform, educate, or enlighten the people in your audience, give them facts, information, details, statistics, and data.*

• *If you're funny, practice your jokes or funny stories.* If you're not naturally funny, don't miss the fifth step in practicing (see Chapter 5). An entertaining speech is the most difficult kind of speech to give. If you're not funny, and try to be, you'll flop.

• *Use a lot of "we" and "you" instead of "I" to be more inclusive, but look at the "you's" carefully; sometimes they should be turned into "we's."* For example, "When *you* are worried, *you* think about your problems" sounds like you're lecturing and criticizing. If you use "we"—"When *we* are worried, *we* think about our problems"—you've allied yourself with your audience, which doesn't seem so superior.

• *Use the imperative.* Useful techniques to use for motivational speakers. "Go that extra mile."

• *Know the definitions of the words and phrases.* Be sure you use the correct word or phrase. Know the difference, for example, between *appraise* and *apprise, disinterested* and *uninterested,* and *hone in on* and *home in.*

The late Malcolm Baldrige, a former secretary of commerce, had such a fetish about words that he issued edicts telling the employees which words they had to eliminate from their letters, memos, and mouths. He especially hated redundancies such as *enclosed herewith, end result, future plans* (what other kinds of plans are there?), *important essentials, new initiatives, personally reviewed, serious crisis, very unique.*

If you're going to use foreign words, be sure you know what they mean. When President John F. Kennedy told the people living in Berlin that he was one of them—"Ich ben ein Berliner"—he really told them that he was a jelly doughnut; *Berliner* is the name for this popular snack.

The Dont's

• *Avoid irrelevant or boring details.* If you use them, you'll lose your audience, and they won't get whatever message you wanted them to have.

• *Don't use technical terms with a nontechnical audience.* And avoid jargon with people outside your field who do not understand your verbal shorthand.

• *Avoid abbreviations or acronyms,* unless *everyone* in the audience is familiar with them. The acronym *ATM* means *Automatic Teller Machine* to the general public, *Asynchronous Transfer Mode* to the telecommunications crowd, and *Acetone Toluene Methanol* to a group of chemists.

• *Don't use clichés.* Avoid hoary expressions like these: *Last, but certainly not least; It's a great pleasure to be here; Without further ado,* and *Here's a person who needs no introduction.* Clichés make you sound like everyone else. Wouldn't you rather stand out a bit?

• *Don't include information you can't verify, don't want to be reminded of in the future, or don't want to hear on radio or television or see in print.* Your credibility is on the line.

Consider this cautionary tale: *I've watched the eyes of a gruff, grey-haired businessman grow wet as he spoke of having to lay off people who'd kept his small shop running for years. I've seen worry in the face of a farm worker idled by a killer arctic freeze. And I've seen the kindly face of a carpenter who couldn't find work framing houses and makes children's toys for free.*—California Governor Pete Wilson

When the press tried to find these people, Governor Wilson had to admit that none of them existed, that they were composites of people he had met. Any goodwill or trust he had built up went out the window.

• *Don't use qualifiers.* Stay away from these words and phrases: *I think, I believe, it seems to me, really, mostly, generally,* and *probably.* They weaken sentences and make you sound wishy-washy.

We will probably win the Super Bowl. NO. *We WILL win the Super Bowl!*

I believe we are honest. Well, are you or aren't you? If you are, say, *We are honest!*

• *Don't use words that aren't words.* Such as "irregardless." They make you sound illiterate.

• *Don't use words you can't pronounce properly.* Former Secretary of Defense Caspar Weinberger says *nucular* for *nuclear.* President Gerald Ford called the dreaded disease sickle cell anemia "sickle cell armenia." The 1988 Democratic presidential candidate Michael Dukakis made a two-syllable word *judg-ment* into a three-syllable word, *judg-jah-ment*. His speechwriters always substituted the words *determined, opinion,* and *conclusion,* instead. Republican Don Young of Alaska always said "Bladderdash" (instead of balderdash). Realtor has two syllables; it is not pronounced *re-la-tor.* And *recognize* has a "g"in it; it is not pronounced *reckanize.*

WIIFM Is Not a Radio Station

The whole time you're speaking, the audience will be asking, consciously and unconsciously, "WIIFM—What's In It For Me?" It will listen attentively if you or the topic is interesting or the delivery is engaging. If not, it will tune you out. It wants to be educated, recognized, inspired, given some tips of the trade and something to take away.

Most important—your listeners want you to make them feel good about themselves and what they do. No matter the reason you're giving the presentation, people in audiences love to be complimented.

Titles

A speech doesn't always need a title, but if you do want to use one, this always grabs an audience: "How to ———— so that you can ————"!

Here's a good example. A speaker talking about the Malcolm Baldrige Quality Award divided his speech into topics: Much Ado About Nothing, A Midsummer Night's Dream, Measure for Measure, The Comedy of Errors, As You Like It, and All's Well that Ends Well! The audience appreciated his cleverness, which unified the speech for them and helped them follow his ideas.

Transitions and Bridges

Transitions or bridges or segues are phrases that signal to the audience that you're changing the subject, that you're going from one point to the next. For example:

Let me shift gears for a moment.

They help move the speach along and help audiences change the subject and anticipate where you're going.

Enough of the past; let's look at the future.

> **Good transitions can make a speech more important to the audience because they feel they are being taken to a positive conclusion without having to travel a bumpy road.**
>
> **—Anonymous**

Transitions take you from the opening to the first point (*Let's first take a look at . . .*), from point to point (*Moving on to the second point . . . ; Our third point is . . . ; Now let's turn to . . . .*), from the last point to the question-and-answer segment (*I've done all the talking. Now I want to know what's on your mind. Let's stop here so I can take some of your questions.*), and from the question-and-answer segment to the closing (*Let me review; Looking ahead five years . . .*).

Make the transitions smooth. You must "take the audience by the hand" to change the subject. For example:

> *Let's take a look at . . .*
> *Look at it another way . . .*
> *In addition, . . .*
> *Enough of———; let's take a look at———.*

Minisummaries work well, too:

> *So far we've talked about the North, the South and the East; now let's turn to the West.*

> *We've talked about care and advocacy. I want to tell you about the research being done here.*

A useful tip: Prepare a list of transitions to have handy during your speech in case you get stuck. Include phrases like: "As I was saying . . . ," or "Once again . . . ."

WRITING FOR A HOSTILE AUDIENCE

Organizing and writing a speech for a hostile audience is different from writing one for a friendly audience. How you get to your objective, the route you take to your destination, is different.

Let's say you want to build a halfway house in or near a residential neighborhood. Most other neighborhoods in the city have a similar facility, but this particular neighborhood is totally opposed to it. The people in the audience don't want or care about what you want. They care about themselves, their families, their health, and their pocketbooks. To get through to this unfriendly audience, follow these steps:

1. First, lay out the problem, giving some history. Don't mention the need for a halfway house in their backyard—yet.

2. Tell of successes with other halfway houses in other parts of the city, county, state, and country. Every sentence must be impartial and neutral. No word, phrase, or sentence should inflame. Explain the need for a halfway house simply and objectively.

3. Recognize and verbally express the audience's objections, one by one, verbatim if possible. (This is a good idea, even if the audience is mildly against your views or issues.) Start with the strongest objection. By recognizing your listeners' agenda and their objections, you surprise them by demonstrating that you have listened to them and considered their reasons and arguments. You begin to disarm them and, in some cases, befriend them.

4. Refute each objection with evidence and counterarguments, preferably outside evidence from third-party authorities who are respected by the audience. Explain why what the audience wants won't work or isn't a good decision or position.

5. Announce your position or solution, and offer basic evidence (i.e., sound, cogent reasons for feeling/thinking the way you do) to support that point, *keeping the audience's needs and wants in mind*. Remember, your audience, like all audiences, is saying, "WIIFM?" You don't want it to tune you out.

6. Finish with a short, memorable conclusion or phrase that captures your position and that the audience can use to persuade itself later.

If it doesn't fit, you must acquit.

Rosa Parks sat down so we could stand up.

One way to look at a hostile audience is to consider a number line from 0 to 10.

0   1   2   3   4   5   6   7   8   9   10

The numbers 0 to 2 represent those diametrically opposed to your view who will never be convinced or persuaded to change their minds. There's little use trying to reach them. The pro-choice people will never convince the pro-life people to change their minds about abortion and vice versa. The numbers 8 to 10 are those who agree with you; often there's no point in preaching to the choir. There are, however, several issues about abortion, for example, about which some people in the middle on abortion—the 3s to 7s—haven't decided, such as issues involving rape, incest, and health of the mother. These are the audience for arguments and persuasion. Be very clear who your audience is as you put together your presentation for a hostile audience.

Using Numbers

When speakers use a lot of numbers, The audience almost always slumbers.

—Charles Osgood

Nothing makes an audience's eyes glaze over faster than numbers (Figure 8). If you're an economist, a financial analyst, or someone who has to use numbers in your presentations, be sure you use visual aids such as slides, overheads, charts, an easel and pad, or handouts so that the audience can *see* what it's *hearing*, which increases retention. If you don't have to use numbers but throw them in because you think they are interesting, keep them to a minimum, and make sure they have lots of zeroes. Round off numbers whenever you can—say *almost a million* instead of *997,755.*

Figure 8.   Numbers are death!

The secret of being boring is to tell everything.

—Voltaire

Proclaim not all thou knowest.

—Benjamin Franklin

Use *two decades* for *21 years*. If an aspirin in a hospital is marked up 198 percent, say *almost 200 percent*.

If you use too many numbers, the audience will get confused and tune you out, and you lose it. For example:

> *The average wage earner in 1950 worked 94 minutes to buy food that can be bought today with just 60 minutes' work.*

LENGTH OF SPEECH

You can't include everything in one speech, nor do you want to. The more you say, the less the audience remembers. If you give the audience too much information or your messages are not focused, the audience will get very little, if anything, because it will tune you out. (A speech is like feeding a baby. If there's too much food on the spoon, the extra food doesn't make it into the baby's mouth—it ends up on its face.) If there's too much information, it won't penetrate. The best way to have a good speech is to have a

A good speech is short and simple. A great speech is shorter and simpler.

good beginning and a good end and have them close together!

Leave out irrelevant details that won't interest the audience. When you buy a car, you don't care how it got there, just what it can do for you. A speech doesn't have to be very long. The Gettysburg Address is shorter than what's written on the back of a potato chip bag!

A good length for a presentation or keynote speech is fifteen to twenty minutes (Figure 9) followed by ten to fifteen minutes of questions and answers. The opening is two to three minutes, the body is fourteen to sixteen minutes (if there are three points, each point is five minutes), and the closing is one to two minutes. A fifteen to twenty minute speech is eight to ten pages, typed and double-spaced (eight pages for Southerners, ten pages for New Yorkers; ten to twelve typed lines equals one minute, twelve lines for New Yorkers, ten lines for Southerners). All told, considering all the time it takes to research, organize, write, and practice, it takes be-

Figure 9. Twenty minutes is a good length of time for a speech.

An orator is one who knows that the brain can absorb what the seat can endure.

—Anonymous

Be brief, be sincere, and be seated.

—Franklin Delano Roosevelt

It takes three weeks to prepare a good impromptu speech.

—Mark Twain

tween twenty and forty hours to prepare a twenty-minute speech.

If you are speaking at a breakfast meeting, be succinct; some people are groggy, and most are eager to get to work and on with the day. If you're speaking at lunch, make sure you don't go past 2 o'clock, which is the nth hour for luncheons, speakers and all. If your turn to speak begins at 1:50 P.M., *cut!* If you're the last speaker on a panel and the speaker(s) before you talked longer than their preallotted time, be prepared to cut your presentation. It may not be fair, but the audience will like you best! If you're speaking at or after a dinner, it's usually a good idea to keep it short. Many of the attendees may be tired at the end of the day, and some may have had a drink or two and want to stay in that "relaxed" mood.

If you're asked to speak longer than twenty to thirty minutes, consider the request carefully before accepting. The speaker who comes to a meeting prepared to talk and talk and talk has not learned the basic lesson of the television-tamed audience: "It had better be more than just a talking head." One way to take up more time is to use videos; another is to involve the people in the audience in an interactive exercise or a game or have them take a questionnaire and then report on their answers. You can also have them break into discussion groups and later share the group discussions. If you can comfortably engage an audience for longer than twenty minutes, you can agree to it. But if you don't have enough material to go longer and keep the audience's interest, decline. Your presentation, like life, is about your looking good. Just because the sponsoring organization has an hour to fill doesn't mean *you* have to fill it. If you can turn your speech into a workshop where everyone learns, by all means, grab the opportunity.

One speaker had her audience pair up for an exercise. She had one person of the two talk for five minutes with "coaching" from the other person; then they switched roles. Then, one at a time, a few stood up to share their experience.

The three worst things to do in the world are: Kiss a girl leaning away from you, climb a wall leaning toward you, and give an after-dinner speech!

—Winston Churchill (Figure 10)

Figure 10.   Three of the worst things to do in the world (according to Winston Churchill).

Kiss a girl leaning away from you.

Climb a wall leaning toward you.

Give an after-dinner speech.

Presentations that are informative and interactive are the most fun. Audience involvement usually makes for a friendlier, participatory learning environment.

Vaudeville had what it called the "twelve-minute secret," which was that no act lasted longer than twelve minutes! If time is running short, always be prepared to cut.

To make a speech immortal, you don't have to make it everlasting.

INTRODUCTIONS

Before you give a speech, someone will usually request your bio or resumé to both introduce you and to use for promotional reasons. Invariably, information about you will turn

> **An after-dinner speech should be like a lady's dress—long enough to cover the subject and short enough to be interesting.**
>
> **—Anonymous**

up in a program or in your introduction that should have been deleted from your resumé a long time ago. Worse, the introducer may actually read your bio or resumé. This won't happen if you write your own introduction for each event (Figure 11). That way, you control what the audience hears about you. Let's face it—you can't totally trust anyone to write the proper introduction for you from a bio or resumé. No one knows what you want the audience to know about you as well as you do. The best speakers and their agents rarely honor the request to send a bio or resumé; instead, they write an appropriate introduction.

If you're making your presentation to people in your company or organization who know you, there's no need for an introduction, but you might want to give the audience a brief summary of what you're about to discuss and why these people have been asked to your presentation.

Introductions should be short. In most situations, the audience came to hear the speaker, not to hear the introducer go on and on about the speaker. This is an example of what an audience should *not* hear:

Figure 11. Write your own introduction.

> *Joan Smith is (position) at —— Company. Before that she was (position) at —— Company. Before that she was at —— Co. where she held the position of ——. She is married to ——, and they have —— children.* [Gag]

There's a better, more professional way to write an introduction. The first three or four sentences of an introduction "open the door" to your speech. They discuss the issue or subject you will talk about:

> *Some people are afraid of our products and our industry. Because of the media, people don't know how safe they really are and the good that they do. How do we get the word out? What do we say when reporters put a microphone in our face?*

The last three sentences should establish the speaker's credibility:

> *Ms. —— was a TV reporter for ten years at CBS and ABC and is now president of her own firm. Her clients include. . . . She has taught people how to talk to reporters for ten years. Join us in welcoming ——.*

Here's an intro for an official of the U.S. Food and Drug Administration:

> *Most national food and drug administrations, including the U.S. FDA, have many rules and regulations. All foreign companies must follow them to be able to sell their drugs and devices in the United States. After tests and trials and gathering of data, one of the first steps in the United States is the preapproval process. Here to take us through that process, including all the revisions to the applications and regulations, is ——, acting director of the Office of Compliance at the Center for Drug Evaluation and Research at the U.S. FDA. Ms. —— has been at the FDA for more than twenty years. She has two masters' degrees and has twice received the FDA*

Commendable Service Award. Please join me in welcoming Ms. ————.

Localize your introduction, if possible, even if it takes some homework. If you, the speaker, have any connection to the city you're speaking in or the organization you're talking to, mention it.

Be sure to tell the person introducing you that you'll be writing your own introduction, and fax it to him or her. This may surprise you, but the introducer will be delighted not to have to write it. It's one less thing he or she has to do. Take an extra copy with you to the speech.

If you're asked to introduce someone else, be sure you can pronounce the person's name correctly. Call the speaker to find out who he or she is, what the speech is about, and how it ties into the program.

Worksheet 9: Write Your Introduction

Write an introduction here for you to use with your next speech. If you don't have a speech coming up, you might pretend you'll be speaking to people in your industry about either your most recent project or your department's.

_____

_____

_____

_____

_____

_____

_____

_____

CHAPTER 4

USING AUDIOVISUAL AIDS

Audiovisual aids are used to illustrate, clarify, and simplify presentations. (Figure 12.) They can enhance your presentation or ruin it. They can *enhance* it by:

- Simplifying complex material.
- Adding variety.
- Supplementing or replacing lecture notes (which means that if you know your opening and closing,

Figure 12. Some examples of audiovisual aids.

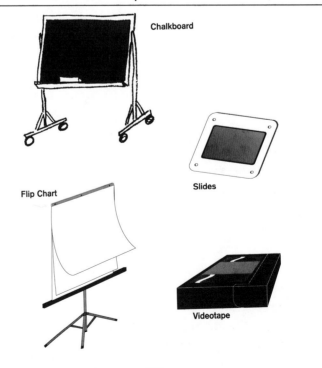

Chalkboard

Slides

Flip Chart

Videotape

you can get in front of a group without a single piece of paper!).

- Clarifying certain points.
- Reducing the time it takes to present a (difficult) concept.
- Increasing retention.

They can *ruin* it if they're:

- Overused
- Confusing
- Too wordy
- Too crowded
- Colorless
- Boring
- Not in sync with the needs of the audience
- Word-for-word what you are saying or if you read them to the audience
- Not handled smoothly
- A lot of boring charts

Presenters who use visuals are perceived as better prepared, more professional, more persuasive, more credible, and more interesting than those who don't.

The time to produce visuals such as slides and overheads is *after* you've written your presentation—not before. The speech determines the visuals; the visuals should never determine the speech.

THE BASIC RULES OF USING AUDIOVISUALS

Audiences remember 40 percent more of what they hear *and* see than of what they only hear. Retention increases threefold (from 14 percent to 40 percent) when listeners *see* as well as *hear*. When visuals were used in teaching one course on vocabulary, learning improved 200 percent.

Many speakers start with the overheads or slides they wish to use and plan their presentations accordingly. This may seem the easiest way to proceed, but effective speechwriting and speechmaking are not about ease. They're about getting your message across in the most effective way. Doing that starts with knowing your audience and carefully figuring out what you want it to know (your objective). Picking the slide first is like putting on the first piece of clothing you see in your closet regardless of where you are going or with whom! You may have clothes on but not the most effective ones. Would you wear a tennis dress to a ball?

Visuals should be simple and express a single idea. They should include only information from your speech. Use as few words as possible—some experts say twelve words, others say not more words than you'd find on a T-shirt or a bumper sticker! All printing, writing, and diagrams should be large and legible, with no crowding, and viewers should be able to understand them in five to twenty seconds. Use handouts to communicate any detailed information.

Never begin or end a speech or presentation with a visual. "Title" slides should be visible only before the presentation starts so that audiences will know they're in the right room or can get an idea what the presentation will be about. If you use a title slide, put a blank slide in just after it and click to it before the program begins. This blank stays in throughout your opening.

Put a red dot in your speech or notes to denote where visuals appear. Keep your audience in mind as you choose and produce your visuals. Don't show a business video to an audience of schoolteachers if you're imploring them to get more computers in the classroom. Instead, show videos or visuals that are of interest to them; they should focus on how other teachers are using computers in the classroom or on other relevant subjects. Words, videos, and props that are not related to your objective and that don't meet your audience's needs are a waste of precious time.

Never read visuals to your audience or repeat word for word what's on the visual; maintain as much eye contact as possible with your audience.

Don't talk to your visual. Don't look at the slide, overhead, projector, flip chart, or blackboard while you're explaining what's on the visual to your audience. Furthermore, don't talk when you're looking down at your notes or when you're not facing your audience. Talk only when your mouth and your eyes are facing the audience. It's perfectly okay to have a few seconds of dead air while you look down at your notes or catch a glimpse of the slide before you talk about it.

When your mouth is not facing your audience, you'll be heard or understood poorly, if at all. If you're wearing a microphone, you may be heard, but many people prefer to *see* your mouth as well as hear you.

Visuals are one more way you help yourself command the audience's attention.

YOUR MULTIMEDIA OPTIONS

RATING SYSTEM KEY

↑ Recommended
↓ Not recommended

↓ *Chalkboards (black or green) and whiteboards*

Pros: Speaker can write an idea or difficult-to-spell words on the board.
Cons: Effective only with small groups; no eye contact since your back is to the audience; your hands get dirty, the chalk squeaks, and the eraser always drops to the floor! Flip charts that can be prepared before the presentation are a better choice.

↓ *Computers*

Pros: If you have the budget for the right equipment, know how to use it, and have practiced, computers are very effective. You can change the order of displays, change the message, and use animation.

Cons: If you don't have the right equipment or you don't know how to use it, the subliminal message will be that you don't have your act together.

Advice: Don't use a computer in your presentations until you learn how to use it correctly. Even if you are an expert, run through your presentation with the computer set up as you will use it. It's better to make your mistakes before you're in front of the audience.

✦ *Flip Charts*

Pros: Flip charts can be effective if they're prepared ahead of time and someone else is flipping the pages for you (or you have a good "baseball" arm and can flip the pages while maintaining eye contact with your audience); they're also inexpensive.

Flip charts can be effective when you need to elicit information from the audience. To begin, you can display the ground rules for the discussion. Then you can record major points expressed by audience members.

Flip chart pages can be torn off and hung up during a meeting. (Think ahead by bringing tape if you are planning to do this.)

Pre-prepared charts can be used from front to back or in reverse.

Cons: Effective only with small groups. You will have no eye contact with the audience if you need to turn your back to write on the chart during the presentation.

Advice: Prepare pages ahead of time. Don't waste the audience's time writing or drawing anything *during* the presentation that can be prepared ahead.

- Tab the pages so that you can find them easily during the presentation.
- Make entries brief. Don't write so much on the same page that it gets cluttered and difficult to read.
- Print clearly in large lettering.
- Use a variety of blue, purple, brown, and black mark-

ers that can be seen from the back of the room (red, orange, and green are hard to see from a distance).

↑ *Maps*

Pros: Maps can be interesting graphics to display during a presentation. A map is really the only way to display geographical information, such as the proximity of a proposed hazardous waste incinerator to a school yard or the commuting routes of an urban area?

Cons: It can be difficult to find a map that can be seen from the back of the room. Make sure the one you use is large enough.

Advice: Use a pointer to help you maintain eye contact with your audience while you're explaining the map. If your map is complex, try to leave it up longer than you might display a simple chart so that your audience can completely digest it.

Microphones

You may need a microphone to be heard by everyone. There are four types of microphones:

Microphones attached to the podium or lectern "tie" you to the microphone. Some mikes are so sensitive that they don't amplify your voice if you move even a few inches away from them.

↓ *Hand-held microphones* à la roving reporters usually have long cords you can trip over, and they leave you with only one hand free (which should be used to gesture, not to hold papers).

Lavaliere microphones clip onto your clothing and leave both your hands free, but they have cords you can trip over if you walk and talk at the same time.

↑ *Wireless microphones* are easiest to use, but make sure, if you can, that you don't sound "tinny."

Pros: The pros here are fairly obvious. A microphone can allow you to be heard by a much larger audience without raising your voice.

Cons: Feedback and distortion that annoys the audience or possibly hurts the ears can certainly be a turnoff. Large microphones, if not positioned correctly, can block the face of the speaker. Nightmare of nightmares, the mike can go out and leave you with an audience that is too large for you to be heard, even if you scream at the top of your lungs.

Advice: Experiment with various microphones so that you have some familiarity with all of them and can judge which one you like best. Request that type when asked and know that you may not always get it. Have a second choice in case your first choice is not available, but know how to use all kinds.

Find time to do a sound check before your audience arrives. Adjust the sound level and the position of the microphone to avoid any embarrassing moments later on.

Remember that the microphone is always "live." Make sure it's off when you're not speaking to the group—before your presentation, during breaks, and after. Don't get caught the way President Reagan did when he said, "My fellow Americans, I am pleased to tell you that I've signed legislation that will outlaw Russia forever. We begin bombing in five minutes." He didn't know the mike was on. Nor did he know the microphone was on when he called the Polish government "a bunch of no-good bums" during a sound check, or when he said that "the world was going to hell" during another mike check.

There are other horrifying examples of mike bloopers. Bozo the Clown, on his daily television show, once said to the viewing children on a Friday just before the show closed, "Be good little boys and girls, and mind your parents, and don't forget to brush your teeth, and I'll see you on Monday." Then he said, "That should hold the little bastards," not knowing his mike was still on—but it was.

"Well," said President Richard Nixon to the television interviewer David Frost before an interview in 1976,

"Did you do any fornicating this weekend?" This gem was heard from coast to coast.

Then there's the speaker who forgot his wireless mike was on when he went to the men's room.

↑ Overheads (TRANSPARENCIES OR VIEWGRAPHS)

Pros: Overheads can be made and changed quickly, easily, and relatively inexpensively, and they can be seen in normal room light.

Cons: They are less professional than slides and can be confusing when they contain too much information. They are also a little tricky to put on straight (Figure 13), and the bright light between overheads can be annoying. In addition, the machine can be noisy, and it's often in (some of) the audience's line of sight.

Advice: If you're going to use overheads, tape a ruler to the top of the glass so that at least the top of the overhead will be on straight. Get used to the overhead's mirror image so that you'll know whether to move the overhead to the

Figure 13. Put your overheads on correctly.

right or left to make it straight. Learn how to cover the bright light that shines between overheads by taping a card to the light and flipping it over between overheads. (You can also turn the machine off.)

Never put a page of text or a page from a book on an overhead. It's too small to be seen, no one will read it, and no one wants to be read to. The moment a page of text appears is the moment the audience, in unison, tunes you and it out!

Use words at least $1/2$-inch high (54- to 72-point type) to make sure that every word of your overhead can be seen from all parts of the room.

If you want the audience to understand a graph, use no more than two or three lines on it. If you want the audience just to see a trend, you can use more. Limit pie charts and bar graphs to seven pies or bars, and place labels *outside* each wedge or bar.

↑ *Props*

Pros: Using props can be very effective because they can make a presentation more interesting.

Con: Props have to be big enough to be seen by the entire audience. Props that have been used effectively include newspapers with big headlines, products like smoke detectors, waste baskets filled with bad press releases, and bad toys. Whether a particular prop will be big enough depends on the size of the audience and the size of the room.

↑ *Slides*

Pros: Slides can be very effective and professional.

Cons: Relatively expensive ($13–30) per slide—often too much information, wrong colors used, kept up too long.

Advice: Slides should be simple and express only one thought or idea. They should have at most six words per line and six lines per slide.

Once you start slides (or overheads, for that matter), you either have to keep changing them or put a blank (black) one in when what you're saying is not related to the visual aid. Bottom line: You never want your audience to see one thing and hear another. It's too confusing. Make sure all your slides are numbered and are either all horizontal or all vertical, not mixed. (The usual format is horizontal; text and diagrams are easier to read that way.) Once the slides are in the tray, click through them quickly before your presentation to be sure they are loaded in the right order, right side up, and focused. Use a magic marker to mark the tops of all the slides. That way you'll always know which way is up when putting them in the tray.

If you have several related messages (e.g., six ways to open a speech), consider using "build" slides (Figure 14). These reveal information gradually for effective communication. You can use two, three, or six build slides to control the message; for example, you can use two slides, with three items on the first slide and all six items on the second slide; or you can use three slides with two items on the first, four items on the second, and all six items on the third (Figure 14); or you can have six slides with one item on the first slide, two items on the second, and so on. If you put the whole list on one slide, the audience will read the whole slide as soon as it sees it. You could

Figure 14.   Use "build" slides.

be standing there naked and the audience would read the whole slide!

If you decide to use slides, here are five tips:

1. Make sure you use colors that can be seen with the lights on.
2. Limit the amount of information.
3. Carry a spare projector bulb.
4. Make sure the projector is on a table or cart that is solid.
5. Use a long pointer or a flashlight arrow if there are fine points you want the audience to see (telescoping or laser pointers can be expensive), but be careful not to wave the pointer around when you're not using it.

✦ Video

Pros: Videos can help the pacing of the presentation by breaking it up and can help support your presentation visually with what can't be shown or done in person.

Cons: Videos can be very expensive to produce ($2,000–$3,000 per finished minute). If you try to create a budget (low-cost) video, it will show, and your presentation will look amateurish.

Advice: The video should be produced professionally. The material should be visually interesting and move at a good pace. An ideal length for many videos is five to seven minutes. If you bought or borrowed a video that is not all that interesting, either use only a portion of the video or don't use it at all—it could ruin the flow of your presentation.

Videos must be large enough to be seen by the entire audience. This means having a large screen, rear projection, or two or more VCRs scattered around the room, depending on the size of the room.

Be sure you are able to make your speech or presentation without your video without the audience's knowing the difference. What if the VCR was not ordered, or it isn't working, or it isn't available, or you forgot to bring your video?

PART II

DELIVERING YOUR PRESENTATION

If you can possibly help it, *don't read your speech* (Figure 15). Listening to someone read a speech is as exciting as listening to someone recite the phone book. There's usually no passion, no excitement, no enthusiasm, no emotion—none of the qualities that help you get and keep an audience's interest. If you read your speech to the audience or speak in a monotone, you will be boring, listening will become a chore, and few people will listen to you. To keep that from happening and to get raves, you must practice.

Figure 15.   You'll sink your presentation if you read your speech.

CHAPTER 5

GETTING YOURSELF READY

PRACTICE, PRACTICE, PRACTICE

There are few natural-born, gifted speakers in the world. Those you think of as being great practiced for years and years. Dr. Martin Luther King, Jr., started preaching when he was a child. Congressman John Lewis admits to practicing on the chickens on his farm when he was growing up. "I could make them bow their heads, but I never could get them to say 'Amen,' " he reports.

Just because you can talk doesn't mean you are a dynamic, outstanding speaker. To be good at anything (tennis, skiing, bridge, bowling) requires practice. The most polished, smoothly delivered, spontaneous-sounding presentations are the result of many hours of practice.

> **The most effective antidote for stage fright is total, slavish, monkish preparation.**
>
> —Jack Valenti, former speechwriter for President Lyndon Johnson and president of the Motion Picture Association of America

Practice improves the speaker's familiarity with the speech and increases confidence. President Ronald Reagan freely admitted that he practiced his speeches five times. If you are **not** prepared—if you do not practice—you will:

- Blink your eyes repeatedly.
- Grope for words.
- Ramble, stumble, or say anything that pops into your head.
- Say "uh" too many times.
- Lose your place.
- Fumble your words, all of which confuses the audience.

A patent attorney who had a case before the U.S. Supreme Court several years ago practiced his argument many times

The more prepared you are, the less worried you'll be. The more prepared you are, the more effective you'll be. The less prepared you are, the more worried you'll be. The more worried you are, the less effective you'll be. If you're going to be effective, it's important not to worry. If you don't prepare, you will worry.

in front of eight bottles on a shelf (there were only eight justices at the time). He also practiced answering those questions he was sure each justice would ask. He won the case!

THE FIVE FOOLPROOF STEPS IN PRACTICING

CAUTION: These steps take time.
GUARANTEE: They work.

Step 1: Type Your Presentation

Type or write out your entire presentation, every word. Make sure every page of your speech ends with a period. While you're practicing, you don't want to be in the middle of a thought when you turn the page.

To keep from losing your place when you're practicing, type your speech double- or triple-spaced with wide (two-inch) margins. Use large type—at least 18-point—upper- and lower-case letters. When you look down, you will be able to see a whole sentence or a whole thought, which will allow you to have more eye contact with the audience and to sound more familiar with the material, which will make you more convincing. Do not type your speech in all caps. They're too hard to read.

Step 2: Read Your Presentation Out Loud

The second step in practicing is to read your presentation *out loud*, slowly, from beginning to end, with a pen or pencil in hand. Reading it silently to yourself does *no* good.

You should eventually sound conversational, as if you were talking over a back fence or across the kitchen table. You should sound like you're talking *to* or *with* your audience, not *at* it.

Change jargon to easy-to-understand words unless every person in the audience will know the lingo. Change hard-to-pronounce words to simpler words. Make sure all words and phrases make sense and are related to your objective. For you to be effective, your audience has to know exactly what you're talking about at all times. If you use words or phrases that people in the audience don't readily understand, they will miss the next words or sentences as they try to figure out what you just said. If you're worried about jargon and words that are hard to understand, read your speech to someone who doesn't work with you or share your expertise, and have him or her stop you every time you use any word or phrase that he or she doesn't readily understand.

As noted earlier, no sentence should have more than twenty words. You'll have to count the words in every sentence to be sure. When you encounter a sentence that has more than twenty words, either shorten it or make it into two sentences. Sometimes—make it rarely—a sentence will be so difficult to edit:

> *These new networks, using advances like fiber-optic lines and digital compression, will move information at least 1,000 times faster than today's phone lines.* (25 words, so we added pauses.)

that the best you can do is find a place to pause. To sound natural, write (PAUSE) and put a comma wherever you plan to stop briefly. Now try reading the sentence.

> *These new networks* (PAUSE), *using advances like fiber-optic lines and digital compression* (PAUSE), *will move information at least 1,000 times faster than today's phone lines.*

Keep reading aloud and editing until you have a speech you like. Now is the time to figure out whether or not you will use visuals, and if so, which ones. Either make them now or order them now (see Chapter 4). Back to your presentation, put slashes (/) or write PAUSE where you want to pause, and underline, highlight, or italicize words or phrases you want to emphasize. (More on pausing in Chapter 6.) You can change the meaning of an ordinary sentence simply by changing which word you emphasize. Read these seven sentences aloud, emphasizing the word in boldface to hear the differences.

I never said he stole money.
I never said he stole money.
I ***never*** said he stole money.
I never ***said*** he stole money.
I never said ***he*** stole money.
I never said he ***stole*** money.
I never said he stole ***money.***

As you practice, watch your confidence increase. Ask yourself frequently: Why am I including this? Does it have to do with my objective? Am I being clear? Begin to memorize your opening.

Figuring Out What to Do With Your Hands

There are two acceptable and effective places for your hands and arms while speaking. They are: gesturing and when not gesturing, resting at your sides until you gesture again. Gesturing is good for many reasons:

- It lets off nervous energy.
- It makes you more interesting to watch.
- It makes you look more relaxed and natural.
- It adds emphasis.
- It adds emotion, interest, and vocal variety to your voice.
- It can be used to illustrate what you are saying.

For example, for "The economy is going up," use a hand motion that swings up; for "We talked about California," the right hand and arm go out at a right angle from your body; for "Now let's talk about the East Coast," sweep your hand and arm the other way (toward the East Coast).

Your hands and arms can rest loosely at your side or lightly on (not glued to) the podium, but only in between gestures.

> **The best way to improve a speech is to shorten it.**
>
> —Anonymous

Put your watch on the podium as you begin, to make sure you finish within the time allotted. You'll be terrific.

NO-NO'S FOR HANDS AND ARMS

There are a number of gestures and hand positions that will distract your audience (Figure 16). Avoid these stances:

- Male fig leaf, with hand over hand over the genitals.
- Both hands deep in pockets. You can't gesture and you look like you're uptight.
- Feet shoulder-width apart, hands behind derriere, à la Prince Philip or a soldier standing at ease.
- Female fig leaf, with arms crossed over chest; this body language says "I don't want to be here."
- Hands on your hips or pointing a finger at the audience; looks too bossy.
- Open wound, one hand across chest holding opposite upper arm.

    If you—especially men—put one hand in a pocket, be sure there are no keys or change inside.

Step 3: Practice Your Written-Out Presentation With Three Aids

Now practice your presentation in front of a *mirror*, with a *stopwatch* and a *tape recorder*. Start the stopwatch and turn the tape recorder on as you begin.

Look in the mirror as you're reading to check your facial expression. It's important that your expression communicate that you are receptive and upbeat, rather than angry or distant. Check your posture, your gestures, and your smile (if appropriate) as you read your speech.

Figure 16. No-no's with the hands.

Male Fig
Leaf

Female
Fig Leaf

Both Hands
in Pocket

Hands Behind
Derriere
(Soldier
at rest)

Hands on
Hips: Bossy

Open Wound
(Walking Wounded)

Both Hands
in Pocket

Hands Behind
Derriere
("Soldier at rest"
or "Prince Philip")

Male Fig
Leaf

Female
Fig Leaf
(also says: "I don't
want to be here ....
Stay away from me ...")

Hands on
Hips: Bossy

Open Wound
(Walking Wounded)

Turn off the tape recorder and the stopwatch when you're finished. Did your speech end within the time allotted to you? If your talk is too long, you *must* cut. Don't plan to just speak faster.

As a rule, you can expect to speak 150 to 180 words, or ten to twelve lines of type, in approximately one minute—ten lines if you talk slowly, twelve lines if you speak quickly. If your presentation is five minutes over and you're from the South, you'll have to cut approximately forty-five lines (675 words), or almost two pages; if you're from New York City, you'll have to cut approximately fifty-five lines (825 words), or more than two pages. Nothing takes the place of this crucial step. Editing always makes a speech better.

Listen to the tape of your presentation at home, in the car, while you're exercising. You won't want to do this. We don't like to hear our own voices. "Is that really how I sound?" we ask, aghast. Yes, it is, and people who've heard you all these years still love you! Get over it!

Ask yourself: How did you sound? Did you read too quickly? Or too slowly? Was there emotion, excitement, or enthusiasm in your voice? After you carry out this painful task, your presentation will be 100 percent better than it was on the tape, no matter how (good) you sounded.

There is a closed facial expression that makes you look angry, a neutral facial expression in which the only things that move are the lips, and an open expression, where one's eyebrows are up and you look receptive. You want to look open. (See Figure 17.)

Step 3a: Practice With Your Visuals

If you're using visuals, they should be ready now. Go through your entire speech and write, or change an overhead, or click the slides at the proper time. Make a red mark in your speech when it is appropriate to change the visual.

Figure 17. "Closed" face, "neutral" face, "open" face.

Great speech makers and orators: Prepare, polish, and practice. Practice, practice, practice. Plan, prepare, practice. Prepare, prepare, prepare. Prepare your speech, prepare the room, prepare yourselves.

Step 4: Boil Down Your Presentation to Bullets

You've written your speech, you've spoken it twice, and heard it once. You're starting to know it. It's time to boil down the ten pages of text to message points, or six-word phrases, on 5 × 7 index cards or 8½ × 11 pieces of paper. Number each card or page. Use the tape recorder again, and the stopwatch if your speech is still too long, and practice the entire presentation in front of a mirror again.

Begin to gesture if you haven't done so already. Speakers who gesture are more interesting to watch and listen to. If the situation lends itself, let your passion show and speak from the heart, much like a riveting minister such as Rev. Dr. Martin Luther King, Jr. You'll have the attention of every person in the room. In fact, if you want to see some of the best, most commanding speakers in your area, ask around the African American community for the most riveting pastors, and attend their churches. You'll learn a great deal and enjoy yourself, too!

Listen to the tape again.

The payoff for all this practice is a more confident, more poised you.

Step 5: Have a Dress Rehearsal

The last practice step is to give your presentation, with or without your notes, wearing the clothes you're going to wear, in front of a camcorder or videocamera. Play the tape with a "coach," someone who will be brutally honest. It may be hard to find such a person, but you must.

Are you doing anything annoying or distracting, like pacing or scratching or rubbing your eyes, wringing your hands, playing with your glasses or tie, pointing a finger, or pulling on your ear? Ask yourself the following questions:

- How do you look?
- Do the clothes look the way you thought they would?
- Will your opening grab your audience?
- How is your eye contact?
- Are you looking "around the room" (at the audience) 90 percent of the time?
- Is your facial expression open?
- Are you gesturing?
- Are you interesting throughout?
- Is your closing memorable?

Your posture should be erect but relaxed. Don't lean on or slump over the lectern or podium or grab the microphone.

To keep from swaying back and forth or shifting from one foot to the other, stand on both feet, placed shoulder-width apart, with one foot half a foot in front of the other. You can't sway in this position. Try it. (Figure 18.)

If your presentation includes a question-and-answer segment, practice this, too. To do this, you and your staff should make up a list of questions you could be asked, with the responses. Include questions that are always asked on your subject, questions you enjoy being asked, and questions you hope no one ever asks.

Figure 18. To keep from swaying back and forth, keep one foot half a foot in front of the other.

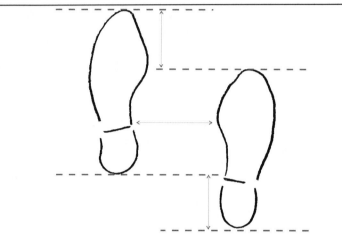

Make sure you know the answers to every possible question. Have your staff or colleagues or friends ask you the questions, on camera if possible, and answer them fully, out loud. Remember how, in the fourth grade, you handed a list of words to your parents the night before a spelling test so that they could test you? This practice amounts to the same thing and is equally important.

Remember the satirist Tom Lehrer's Boy Scouts Marching Song: "Don't be nervous, don't be flustered, don't be scared. Be prepared."

Worksheet 10: Speaker Report Card

To be the best, you have to look on criticism as a gift. As a last practice step, assemble a few people to whom you can make your presentation. Give each attendant a copy of the following, and have them fill it out during and after you speak. Every checkmark is a present to you that, if heeded, can make you an even more dynamic presenter.

Speaker's name: _____

Did the speaker (check all that apply):

____ use gestures?

____ read the speech?

____ appear confident?

____ display passion about the subject?

____ seem frightened?

____ seem comfortable with the audience?

____ use transitions?

____ appear organized?

____ have good eye contact?

____ speak in a clear voice?

____ have a strong grasp of the subject?

____ use technical terms, jargon, or abbreviations you didn't understand?

Was the speaker talking:

____ to you?

____ over your head?

____ in a condescending way?

Were there enough examples, stories, anecdotes?
Yes   No

Can you remember one?   Yes   No

   If so what was it about? _____

_____

Were you distracted by the speaker's clothing or gestures?   Yes   No

What was the purpose of the speech as you understood it?

_____

> **The human brain starts working the mo- ment you're born and never stops until you stand up to speak in public.**
>
> **—Anonymous**

What 3 points did the speaker make?

Point 1: _____

Point 2: _____

Point 3: _____

Did you lose interest in the speech?   Yes   No

If yes, at what point? _____

Did the opening grab you?   Yes   No

Was the close memorable?   Yes   No

Did the speakers use too many numbers?   Yes   No

Was the speech:

_____ too long?

_____ too short?

_____ just right?

_____ boring?

_____ interesting?

Was the speaker's delivery:

_____ animated?

_____ enthusiastic?

_____ boring?

Were audiovisual aids:

_____ relevant?

_____ interesting?

Did the speaker read them?   Yes   No

STAGE FRIGHT

There is bad news and there is good news about stage fright. The bad news is that you will be nervous. The good news is that you will be nervous. Stage fright is a sign of a caring performer. Being flooded with adrenaline and sweating or perspiring (men sweat, women perspire) means, believe it or not, that you want to do a good job. Expect it and accept it.

In every list of fears, the fear of public speaking ranks first, ahead of death. Fear of public speaking is actually three fears—fear of failing or of performing poorly, fear of the audience, since one sees the audience as a judgmental authority, and fear of the material. Fear of public speaking keeps some people from making a good presentation, while it keeps others from ever standing in front of an audience at all.

TOP TEN FEARS

1. Speaking before a group
2. Heights
3. Insects and bugs
4. Financial problems
5. Deep water
6. Sickness
7. Death
8. Flying
9. Loneliness
10. Dogs

Believe it or not, having your pulse quicken and your heart beat faster and experiencing clammy palms, a parched throat, weak, quavering knees, a dry mouth, nausea, dizziness, shaky hands, shortness of breath, tense muscles, tight vocal cords, and an overall ill feeling adds excitement to your entire presentation (Figure 19).

If you're nervous, know that:

- The audience rarely notices your nervousness. It wants to like you and expects you to be a good speaker.
- The audience is receptive. The people in the audience are usually there because they want to be.

Figure 19. Expect and accept nervousness.

- The panic usually passes once you get going (especially if you used the five foolproof steps to practicing).

Your speech will be flat, dull, boring, and lacking in energy unless you have at least a little bit of fear. You should feel not relaxed but stimulated and excited. And if you do feel relaxed, get some fear!

Keeping Your Fear in Check

Although a little fear is energizing, you don't want to be paralyzed by extreme fear, so here are some tips to keeping it under control.

Try to think positive thoughts, like these:

I can succeed.
I'm glad I'm here.
I'm glad you're here.
I care about you.
I know my subject.

Don't show, share, or talk about your fear. Act and appear confident. "Fake it till you make it" if you have to. If you're well prepared, you will perform well. If you've followed the five foolproof steps to practicing, the fear and the nervousness will go away within the first minute of starting to speak.

If your fear is overwhelming, there are several ways to relieve stress and control anxiety:

1. *Walk up and down stairs.*

2. *Do isometric exercises.* Tighten and hold selected muscles in parts of your body (hands, feet, stomach) for several seconds, then relax and let go; the tension usually disappears.

3. *Breathe deeply.* Take a deep belly breath through your nose, inflating your abdomen until it protrudes. Hold for a count of three, and breathe out through your mouth, contracting your abdomen. This increases the flow of oxygen, which stimulates the brain and relieves stress. Repeat.

4. *Yawn a few times to loosen the jaw.*

5. *Exercise* (Figure 20). The singer Harry Belafonte has been known to do cartwheels before his performances.

6. *Meditate.* Go into a corner, close your eyes, and erase all thoughts and pictures from your mind. If anything pops in, erase it. A minute of this helps; two is better.

7. *Visualize.* Some speakers use visualization to lower anxiety and ensure success. The night before the presentation, they close their eyes and visualize themselves giving their talk from beginning to end. When they actually make their presentations, it's like giving it for the second time, and they're terrific! (Figure 21.)

There are also a few things you should *not* do:

1. *Don't drink alcohol.* Alcohol does not relax you, and it clouds your thinking. If you have a drink, you won't perform as well. In fact, you will do all those things you would have done had you not prepared at all, like losing your place and fumbling.

Figure 20.   Exercise to control anxiety.

2. *Don't try to get rid of the fear,* because you can't; more important, you don't want to. Remember: Fear is a stimulant that helps you do a better job!

The Week and Day of Your Speech

The week of your presentation, read the newspaper and/or listen to the news every day, especially on the morning of your speech. If there is anything in the news that is relevant to the group you're speaking to, mentioning it will add to your credibility. Or you might be asked a question about something in the news, and you want to be able to answer it.

If you are the luncheon or dinner speaker at a half- or all-day meeting and your schedule permits, attend all or part of some of the sessions prior to yours. This will give you a

Figure 21.   Visualize giving a great speech, and you will!

better sense of the organization and its issues, and you may want to make a comment on something you saw or heard, which can further add to your credibility.

Try to get in a workout or a brisk walk the day of your speech. Exercise will help calm you down.

CHAPTER 6

SHOWTIME

It's finally time to see how all the preparation and practice really pay off. But this is no time to get casual. There's still plenty of work to be done to lock in success.

APPEARANCE

Effective communication involves five elements: appearance, facial expression, body language, vocal variety, and information. Studies show that 93 percent of communication is nonverbal. That is, how you look, how you sound, and how you come across are *very* important (Figure 22). These five elements play a major part in determining the degree of impact you have, for better and for worse. Only a small part of the impression you make is based on what you say, whether you're selling something, making a report, asking for funds, arguing with a zoning committee, or confronting an audience via television or radio.

An old but still excellent example of this reality is the first televised presidential debate between John F. Kennedy and Richard M. Nixon, in 1960 in the WBBM-TV (CBS) studios in Chicago. Nixon looked tired, had a 5 o'clock shadow, refused to wear makeup, knit his eyebrows (which made him look angry at worst, not friendly at best), perspired a lot, shifted back and forth from one leg to another (he'd hurt one leg the week before), and wore a light brown suit (against a light background), which made him look wimpy. Kennedy, on the other hand, was handsome and tanned, wore a dark suit that made him look professional and fit, had an open face, and appeared confident. Two cam-

Figure 22. Ninety-three percent of communication is nonverbal.

eras were used to cover the debate. It was customary up to that day for both cameras to focus on the person speaking. On that day, however, for the first time, one camera was on the person speaking and the other was on the person listening. Nixon didn't know this, but Kennedy did. When the camera was on Nixon, he was not looking at Kennedy, and he looked rather bored. When the camera was on Kennedy, he was smiling, and looked at either the studio audience or at Nixon.

When the debate was over, polls indicated that television viewers declared Kennedy the winner, while radio listeners preferred Nixon. When people *saw* Nixon, they didn't like him, but when they *heard* him, they liked what they heard and respected him. It's the only time in history that there has been such a split in public opinion.

You may be very bright and know your subject cold but if you're not likable—if you don't have an open facial expression, make eye contact, and talk *with* the audience—the audience will not listen.

**"No mat-
ter what
you say,
your
clothes
say more."
(Figure
23.)**

To avoid appearing distracted or nervous, watch out for these behaviors:

- Swaying or rocking or pacing
- Thumping or tapping on the lectern or a flip chart
- Staring at the ceiling, the floor, or your notes
- Playing with change in your pockets

Dressing Appropriately

Dress like your audience or one level above it. If the audience is in black tie, you should be, too. If you're speaking in a more casual setting, on a Saturday or at a resort, and everyone is wearing casual clothes, wear the same, with perhaps a sport coat. If you're talking to bankers or lawyers, wear your best business clothes. If you're talking to advertising execs or clothing designers, you can be more creative, but above all, do not wear anything that will distract from your message.

One lobbyist in Washington, D.C., was a real fashion plate. He always wore the latest styles, fabrics, and colors. How-

Figure 23.   No matter what you say, your clothes say more!

49%

ever, he represented successful but unsophisticated small-business owners of stores that sold automotive parts. He found that his clothing was off-putting. He decided to dress more like his clients did and immediately won them over.

All speakers should check a mirror before speaking to be sure that their hair is combed and off the face, the tie or other accessories are straight, and makeup is fresh. They should also check that they're not wearing anything that could distract from their message. If you have on a smashing tie or a gorgeous scarf or dangling earrings or a name badge or if your appearance is unkempt, much of the audience will be distracted and miss some, or all, of what you have to say.

You want to look, sound, and feel your best. Let the audience see you, not your clothing. Since many presentations are made by people in business attire, here are a few guidelines:

Men's Business Attire

- A clean and pressed dark (blue or charcoal gray, not black) suit or sport coat
- A long-sleeved white shirt (pastels, such as light gray or light blue, are best if TV cameras are present, because white can make you look washed out on camera)
- A (boring) conservative or striped red or maroon tie
- Above-the-calf socks (People, especially women, are turned off when they see that piece of skin between the top of a man's sock and the pantleg!)
- Black or brown shined, soled shoes (remember the photo of Adlai Stevenson in 1952 with the hole in his shoe and a similar picture of Bill Clinton in 1992?!)
- A watch and a ring, if worn, but no other jewelry—no tie tack, lapel pin, earrings, necklaces, name tags, or badges—anything that could call attention to itself

Whether the suit or sport coat should be buttoned or unbuttoned depends on whichever makes the lapels lie flat. Vests make men look several pounds heavier.

Women's Business Attire

- A clean and pressed suit or dress with sleeves in a *strong* color (busy patterns and plunging necklines are distracting)
- Knee- to mid-calf length skirt if you will be sitting where others can see your legs before or after the speech, otherwise it can be a bit above the knee
- White blouses (pastel blouses if TV cameras are present)
- Shined, closed-toe shoes with moderate heels (carry an extra pair of hose)
- Conservative, simple jewelry—pearls and/or gold look fine; no diamonds

Women should avoid:

- Pastel or pale-colored suits or dresses (they denote weakness, and you want to look strong and confident; however, a pastel blouse with a strong-color suit is fine)
- Black clothing (it adds ten years and should be saved for a funeral)
- Heavy makeup
- Low-cut neckline
- Large, chunky, dangling bracelets, earrings, or necklaces

ARRIVING AT THE SITE OF YOUR SPEECH

For some of your audience, your speech starts when you arrive, so be aware that people are watching you from that moment. Don't forget to check a mirror both before you enter and before you speak.

Arrive early, for many reasons:

- To make sure you're at the right place in the right room.
- To check out the room. Walk around. Move furni-

ture if you have to. Try out a few of your visuals to be sure they can be seen from all parts of the room. If you're using an easel, center yourself in front of the room and place it slightly to one side. Write on it as you would during your presentation, then go to the back of the room to be sure what you just wrote can be seen.

- To check out the air conditioning or heating system. It may not be working, and you'll need that extra time to adjust the temperature.

- To check out the AV equipment to be sure that everything you ordered is there, that everything is connected correctly, that the projector is focused, and that the TV and VCR work. Be sure that your videotapes are cued up. Brief the person who will be operating the slide projector or VCR if it won't be you.

- To check out the podium and the dais and to know how to get on and off the dais.

- To try the microphone to be sure it works or to learn how it works. Will you have to turn it off and on? If the mike is at the podium, try it out to see where you should put your mouth to be heard but not to blast the audience. If the microphone is a clip-on, find the place on your shirt or jacket that is the most effective place to put it (lavaliere mikes often go at the second button of your shirt or blouse). If it's a wireless mike, clip it on and put the battery and cord in your pocket (or hook the battery onto your belt) as soon as you get it—but make sure the mike is off. You don't want to have to fiddle with the connection at the last minute. Learn how to plug yourself in and turn the mike on when you're ready to speak.

- To check out the lighting. If you're using slides, overheads, or video, experiment with the room's overhead lighting. (The darker the room, the more people will be sleeping.) Be sure you won't be standing in front of a brightly lighted window. (You'll be silhouetted, your face won't be seen clearly, and you'll lose one of the most persuasive tools you have—eye contact.)

- To make sure the markers aren't dried up (if you're planning to use them).
- To find your handouts. If you sent a set of handouts to the host to be copied, make sure plenty of copies are available. If they're not in your room, you may have to look for them or get them copied yourself.
- To chat with the person who'll be introducing you to be sure that he or she has your introduction. If not, give the person the copy you brought with you.
- To talk with the host about how the event or program is going and about the mood of the audience.
- To take a last look in the mirror. You don't want anything (tie askew, messy hair, smudge on your face) to distract from your message.
- To meet the other speakers.
- To meet as many people in the audience as you can. Some speakers stand at the front door and greet the guests as they enter. Others walk around and meet the people who arrived early. It's a way of establishing "friends" in the audience because it's easier to talk to "familiar" faces than to a room full of strangers. It also helps rid you of some of your fear. You may also hear some "local info" you can use in your presentation.

Carry an extra projector bulb, a spare copy of a videotape you plan to show, and an extra marker or two. If you assume that something will go wrong and are prepared for the worst-case scenario, such as having to give your speech without any audiovisual aid, it won't happen.

Don't go over your speech notes or sit and wonder if you prepared enough or if you're going to blow it or wish the speech was over. The audience will perceive your insecurity and wonder about you or, worse, doubt you. Rather, focus on what's going on around you or on anything but your speech. You've practiced it, you know it. Looking at it just before giving it will only make you more nervous.

Make sure you have a glass of water, a handkerchief or a tissue, and a throat lozenge at the podium or wherever you'll be speaking.

If you have notes, keep them with you and take them to the podium. Papers put on the lectern ahead of time have been known to disappear with the previous speaker!

GIVING YOUR SPEECH

You've written your speech. You've practiced it several times. You've heard it several times. You've memorized your opening and your closing. You know it. Even though you may be scared and have butterflies, you're ready to go. Start just the way you've practiced several times. With a smile (or at least an open expression) and 100 percent eye contact to establish a bond with the audience, jump into the opening.

If possible, know your speech well enough to deliver it without any notes. Some experts say that the presence of a piece of paper detracts from credibility.

A good speaker gives the audience seven messages:

1. I will not waste your time (you understand WIIFM—What's In It For Me?).
2. I know who *you* are, and I know why you came (you meet the audience's needs).
3. I am well organized (your message is clearly understood).
4. I will deliver this speech in an interesting, conversational way (to make it engaging for the audience).
5. I know my subject (audiences want to hear experts and authorities).
6. Here are my most important points (you realize it's your responsibility to make sure the audience understands the messages).
7. I am finished (you know you must bring it all together with a solid finish so that the audience feels fulfilled).

> **Good results are seldom led to when people feel they're being read to.**
>
> —Charles Osgood

Never begin by apologizing for anything except being late. Apologizing is an irritating waste of time. Don't share with the audience that you have little or no experience in public speaking or you're not really the best person to speak. It turns people in an audience off and makes them wonder why they're listening to you.

Winston Churchill imagined everyone in the audience naked when he spoke!

If you must read some or all of your speech (say, if you give several speeches a week, there's no time to practice, you can't memorize the open or close, and you can't give the speech from bullets), at least practice in the rest room or in the car on your way so that you become more familiar with your presentation. Underline the words you want to emphasize, and put slashes or write PAUSE where you want to pause. Speakers who never see their speeches before they give them usually sound just that way—as if they've never seen the speeches before. They are not respected or listened to nearly as much as those who (respect the audience enough to) find the time to practice.

Your goal is never to be boring. Remember three things that can help you the most with your delivery: eye contact, smiling or an open face, and passion.

Making Eye Contact

> **If you haven't struck oil in two minutes, stop boring.**
>
> —George Jessel, comedian

Make eye contact with as many people in the audience as often as possible. Aim for making eye contact 90 percent of the time. Eye contact (and gesturing, having an open face, and passion) do more to help your delivery than anything you say or anything else you do. Having good eye contact establishes a positive relationship with the audience and demonstrates confidence and sincerity.

Look at individuals in all parts of the audience—left, center, right, front and back. Look right in their eyes—not at their forehead or the tops of the heads in the back row. (Figure 24.)

Figure 24. Eye contact is very important.

Don't forget to look at your audience 100 percent of the time for both your opening and your closing. Use your eye contact to establish a bond with the audience.

I don't object to people looking at their watches when I am speaking. But I strongly object when they start shaking them to make certain they are still going.

—Lord Birket (1883–1962)

If you have to read all or part of your speech, you can maintain eye contact if you have your speech typed in large type with a three-inch left margin. As you look down, your eye "takes a picture" of several lines at a time. If you must read parts, such as a lengthy quote or highly technical material, cue the audience that you're going to read something, and be sure to look at the audience as often as possible.

Eye contact provides feedback from your audience so you always know how you are doing.

Reading Your Audience

As you move into the body of the speech, begin to read your audience (Figure 25). You can always tell how you're doing by looking at your listeners. If they are sitting upright and maybe a bit forward, eyes alert, looking at you, attentive, smiling, listening, laughing, taking notes—you're doing a great job. You're meeting their needs and holding their interest.

If they are looking at their watches, the floor, or the ceiling, reading, doodling, frowning, yawning, nodding, sleeping,

Figure 25.   Read your audience to see how you're doing.

snoring, or leaving—you're not doing a great job! And it's your fault, not the audience's. It's not that the audience was up too late the night before or had too much to drink or is preoccupied. It's that you're not holding its attention.

If you sense you are losing the audience, there are several things you can do to try to get them back (but it is tough):

- Intensify your eye contact.
- Gesture more; this will be more interesting to watch, and will help vary your voice more.
- Involve the audience—ask questions or ask for comments on what you're talking about.

If you've lost your audience and nothing works to bring them back, put yourself and your audience out of misery by giving highlights of material not yet covered; then jump to your conclusion and get off. And get speaker training.

The Importance of Being Dynamic

Your speech or presentation is a performance. To be dynamic, you must entertain, that is, get and keep the audience's interest and attention throughout. If you are energetic and enthusiastic, the audience will be.

Why don't th' feller who says, "I'm no speech-maker" let it go at that in-stead o' givin' a demonstra-tion?

—Frank McKinney Hubbard (Kin Hubbard) (1868–1920), American humorist

Speak clearly. Don't mumble; enunciate. If you can't or don't speak clearly, you've wasted both your time and the audience's. People in the audience will listen attentively to acquire information if you have power or are conveying important information, but they will escape into doodling and daydreams if the required effort is too great. The audience must be able to hear and understand you.

The proper tone, inflection, and volume create a positive environment. Your delivery is like a piece of music—you must vary the speed and the volume. Not all pieces of music are played at the same speed or decibel level throughout. Good volume and good pacing communicate confidence.

Pausing is an effective technique to use in public speaking. It adds significance to your words, gives the audience time to let an interesting or startling point sink in and to think and anticipate what will come next. Pause when you make a major or shocking point or before a punchline.

Many speakers have to write pauses into their presentations to be sure they remember to stop:

> *There are several types of applications covered under user fees (PAUSE): full NDAs (PAUSE), some paper NDAs (PAUSE), initial antibiotic certification applications (PAUSE), PLAs, and ELAs (PAUSE). Other products not covered are (PAUSE) human blood. . . .*

The audience will wait for you. The late comedians George Burns and Jack Benny used pausing very effectively.

Mugger to Benny: Your money or your life.
[*Benny,* who cultivated the persona of a skinflint, stands in his famous stance, his back to the mugger, arms folded, silent.]
Mugger [impatient, repeats]: Your money or your life.
Benny [slowly turning his head toward the mugger]: I'm thinking.

Pausing gives you time to think and allows the audience to absorb your information. If you pause at the right time in

The most precious things in speeches are pauses.

—Sir Ralph Richardson, actor

the middle of compelling material, the audience will wait eagerly to hear what comes next.

HANDLING THE POTENTIAL PROBLEMS

Here are some tips for handling some of the sticky situations you may encounter:

• *Fumbled words.* If you fumble a word or two occasionally, no big deal. You're not the Lone Ranger. Everyone does it. Just slow down, relax, say the fumbled words correctly, and go on from there. No one will remember that you fumbled a word or two.

LOSING YOUR PLACE

If you stumble, you can:

- Repeat the last statement for emphasis.
- Expand on the last statement with an example or an anecdote that you brought with you for just this occasion.
- Tell an appropriate joke or story.
- Summarize up to that point.
- Admit that you've lost your place, and take a second to find it.

• *Large Rooms.* Speak a little slower than you practiced because it takes time for the words to bounce around a large room.

• *Interruptions.* There is no hard and fast rule about handling interruptions, such as latecomers, coughers, and people who walk out. Either ignore them or wait until the problem passes. A humorous anecdote you've collected ahead of time might be appropriate. If it's a small group and two people are talking, it is certainly appropriate to stop talking and stare

> **I'm here to talk and you're here to listen, and if you finish before I do, feel free to leave.**
>
> **—Adlai Stevenson**

at them until they stop, or keep talking and stare at them, or ask them nicely to stop.

- *TV cameras.* Don't look at them. Forget them and just look at the audience. The microphone is always live, so don't say anything you don't want to see in print, hear on radio or TV, or have quoted back to you.

Here are some do's and don'ts:

- *Don't memorize your speech.* It will sound insincere.

- *Don't leave the lectern the second you're finished speaking.* As the audience is applauding, stand there for a few seconds looking at the audience, acknowledging it acknowledging you. It's a nice touch. Then close your folder or put your cards in your pocket, and walk from the podium. Don't talk to anyone sitting or standing next to you, and stay in eye contact with the audience.

- *Make (intellectual) love to your audience and let it love you back.* And if it does, ask for letter(s) of recommendation, preferably on company stationery. Also ask for suggestions for other places to speak.

REMEMBER:

- If you like your audience, it'll like you.
- Enjoy yourself, and the audience will enjoy itself.
- If you hate (giving) your speech, the audience will not like it either.
- If you are uncomfortable, the audience will be, too.
- If you're bored, the audience will go to sleep.

Dale Carnegie told speakers to act as if there were nowhere else in the world they'd rather be than with that audience sharing their expertise.

QUESTION AND ANSWER: A NEW WAY TO HANDLE IT

The question-and-answer segment is often as or more important than the speech itself. How you look, sound, and come across as you answer the audience's questions can make or break your speech. You want to keep everyone in the audience as engaged and alert as you did during your presentation (Figure 26). The same rules about total eye contact, open expression, gesturing, and meeting the needs and interests of your audience at all times apply during the Q&A.

Your goal in every presentation is to leave your audience with a good feeling about you, your message, your organization, and your industry. Depending on the subject, taking questions *after* a speech can put your goal at risk. What if the last question posed is a negative one or a neutral one? After all your hard work, the audience could walk out feeling nothing, or even feeling angry. It could leave with a negative feeling about you, your message, your organization, and your industry.

Figure 26.   Make Q&A a part of your presentation.

This won't happen if you put the question-and-answer segment *into the speech itself*, after your last point and before the conclusion. This way you control the last thing the audience hears. Here's how it works. You deliver your speech through the body, through the third point and its examples. Then you say something like:

> *I've talked a lot about [the subject of the presentation]. I want to hear what's on your mind.*

Most audiences aren't prepared for the Q&A to come before the end, and they may not be ready with questions. No problem. If no hands go up, you should be prepared with a question to ask yourself. Say something like:

> *The most often-asked question about [subject of speech] is ———.*

Then answer it. The hands will go up.

Here's another way to break the ice. Speaking at the Smithsonian Institution, Ted Koppel of ABC News opened up the question-and-answer segment this way: "No one likes to ask the first question, so who will ask the second?" Hands shot up.

By putting the question-and-answer segment into the speech itself, you also avoid having to announce the last question. You (silently) decide which is the last question and segue to the closing or conclusion whenever *you* want. This way, the last thing the people in the audience hears is your conclusion, telling them what *you* want them to do, think, or feel after hearing you. If you do this right, you'll leave the audience with a good feeling about you, your message, your business, and your industry.

You must prepare for the question-and-answer segment. If you give a dynamic speech but fall down during the Q&A, the audience will be left with its last impression—the negative one. You don't want to get even one question that you don't know how to answer confidently.

Start practicing this make-or-break segment by anticipating and developing a list of questions you could be asked. Don't do this alone. Ask your staff or others to add to the list. They will come up with excellent questions that you didn't think of, no matter how immersed in the subject you are. Some should be questions you always get, some should be those you like to get, and some should be tough, the ones you hope you never get.

Have someone test you by asking you the questions. Make sure you know the answers, and practice them out loud. Practice the question-and-answer segment with several people. Have them fire questions at you so that you can practice answering. Tell them to be tough on you.

If you're worried about the kinds of questions you're going to get, you can arrange for your host to have index cards available. Have the person who introduces you announce that blank cards are available and that people with questions can write them on the cards and submit them to you. Audiences don't much like this, especially if you or your subject are controversial, but it is a way for you to control this important part of your presentation because you have no obligation to answer every question.

Learn how to "bridge," "segue," or "transition" from a sticky question to one of your message points. The phrase "The real issue is . . ." always works. If someone asks you about football and you want to talk about leadership, respond to the question briefly: "I love football, but the real issue is. . . ." Then start talking about leadership.

When there are no more raised hands or people waiting at microphones, or whenever you're ready, transition to your closing. Don't ask if there are any more questions. It makes you appear to be begging and weak. You're the authority, and you want to leave strong. There will always be people who will come up afterward and talk to you one on one.

Some Important Do's and Don'ts

1. Take questions from the whole audience, not just from one or two sections.

2. Listen to each question without reaction; then respond simply and directly. If you acknowledge a question as a "good" question, some listeners may misconstrue your comment to mean that other questions weren't.

3. Don't relax during the Q&A; continue standing straight and gesturing. Remember, you are still "on."

4. When answering a question, don't keep your eye on the person who asked the question the whole time. Begin and end on the questioner, and look at the rest of the audience in between. Staying focused on the questioner leaves the rest of the audience out.

5. After responding to a question, take another question. Don't ask the questioner, "Does this answer your question?" If you haven't answered it satisfactorily, the questioner will:

- Let it pass, in which case you move on.
- Say that you haven't answered the question and ask you to answer it.
- Come up after the speech for a further explanation.

6. If you're in a large room and have to repeat all the questions so that everyone can hear them, repeat all positive questions the way they were asked. Not only will this give the whole audience a chance to hear the question but it will give you a chance to think where you're going with the answer. Always paraphrase negative questions positively.

Negative question: When did you stop beating your wife?
Restatement: This gentleman asked about my wife.

Negative question: Don't you care more about the bottom line than about safety?
Restatement: This person asked about our policy and attitude about safety (*or* our bottom line).

Negative question: Why have so many of your staff been found to be using drugs?
Restatement: This person wants to know about drugs and our staff.

7. Acknowledge negatives, and turn them into posi-
tives.

Negative statement: Your company had the worst complaint
   record in its industry.
Positive answer: I'm not satisfied with even one complaint,
   and we have made progress on handling complaints this
   year.

8. If you're asked about something that you discussed
in your speech or if a question repeats one you were already
asked, say, "We've already gone over that; why don't you
come up afterward, and we'll talk about that." Then—and
this can be tricky—bridge to one of the points you made in
your presentation, turn to the other side of the room, or
take your eyes off the questioner and take another question.
No negotiating, no asking if that's all right. Just do it. You're
in charge.

9. When asked to respond to a charge from an uniden-
tified source, ask for the source. If the questioner doesn't
know it or won't give it, say that you never answer questions without a source but that you'll be delighted to discuss
the subject with him or her after the speech. Then move on
to the next question.

10. If you're asked an irrelevant question or one that is
off the subject, acknowledge the question ("That's an interesting question, but it isn't the subject today"); then invite
the questioner to talk about it later: "Why don't you come
on up afterward, and we'll go over it." Then switch your
eye contact, and take another question.

11. If a disorganized question is asked, state one of your
three points or say whatever you want, and move on.

12. If a questioner goes on and on, you must break in,
nicely, and ask if there's a question. If there isn't a question
after another fifteen seconds or so, break in and say something like, "You're making an interesting point, but we have
other questions to get to. Come on up afterward, and we'll
talk about it." Switch your gaze, and take another question.

You're in charge, and you don't want to sacrifice your whole audience for one person.

13. If you're asked a hypothetical question ("What if . . . ?", "Suppose . . .") answer it only if it's about something you know (e.g., a planned procedure for evacuating an amusement park in an emergency).

Don't get pulled into "reading a crystal ball." Simply say that the question is hypothetical: "No one can see into the future; I do know that . . ." and restate one of your points. You can also say, "I only work with what is, and I know . . ." and restate one of your points. Then turn your body, switch your gaze to someone on the other side of the room, and take the next question.

14. If you are asked multiple questions, it is not your responsibility to remember all of them. Pick one and answer it; then either move on to another questioner or ask the questioner, "What else did you ask?" It's your choice. Usually the person has forgotten what else he or she asked, and you can move on.

15. If you're asked a question to which you don't know the answer, you have two choices: Say you don't know, but you do know where to find the answer and will do so and get back to the questioner, or say that you don't know, but you do know whom to call and then give that person's name and number to the questioner. Don't make up an answer, and don't be afraid to say you don't know.

16. Use sources or studies to bolster your answer: "The latest XYZ poll said. . . ." It adds to your credibility.

17. Stay calm, reasonable, positive, and professional. Don't get mad or argue with anyone in the audience.

PANELS

An effective panel is a group of people brought together to work as a team to meet the needs of the audience. An ineffective (or less effective) panel is a group of individuals who have never seen or talked to one another prior to the event who sit together at a table in front of an audience and "do their own thing."

To achieve some level of team spirit and responsibility, it is important that the moderator arrange a meeting or a conference call with the panelists before the meeting so that they can "meet" each other, determine each participant's role, and decide the order of the speakers (who goes first . . .). The panel will be able to meet the audience's needs better if the members know a bit about each other. If the moderator doesn't or can't do this, it's perfectly okay for a panelist to perform this important task.

It's important to be sure that what's written in the program or brochure clearly reflects what will, in fact, be covered. If you are determining the format of the program, decide whether each panelist will present for a few minutes or will just respond to questions from the audience and/or the moderator. (Each panelist should stake out the area he or she is going to cover. It's upsetting and disconcerting to hear a panelist before you give your speech.)

As moderator, you should find out whether they'll be speaking from their seats at a table or at a lectern. Decide how the question-and-answer segment will be handled—will panelists respond from their seats (the easiest way), or will they go back to the lectern for each question? If panelists will respond from the table, make sure there will be enough microphones. The moderator should be sure to repeat every question.

Also make sure that someone is making the name tent cards and that there are introductions for each speaker. Don't forget to write your own remarks. (It is most effective to introduce each speaker before he or she speaks, rather than all at once at the beginning.)

As a panelist, when you arrive at the event, check out the room and the AV equipment if you're using it, and greet and chat with the moderator and the other panelists (this will give the audience a positive impression of you). If there are no tent cards, see if you can find them, or get cardboard or file folders to make some.

Don't forget to take one last look in the mirror.

If the moderator doesn't give you an adequate introduction, be sure to introduce yourself. When it's your turn, briefly give your credentials and explain why you're there. Observe your time limit. If each panelist is given ten minutes, don't go over, by even a second. Better yet, aim for nine and a half minutes to leave plenty of time for the Q&A. If you have an answer to a question posed to another panelist, don't be shy. Jump in at the end of his or her answer with your response.

If you disagree with another panelist, there are two ways to handle it. You can turn to the other panelist and state your objection, which can lead to a lively disagreement. A more mature way to handle the situation is to tell the audience that you don't agree ("We at RFT Company don't agree with Mr. Jones. We think . . ."), and state your position. Even though some audiences like it when panelists slug it out, it doesn't make either of you look very professional.

To leave the audience with a good impression of you, your issue, your organization, and your industry, arrange ahead of time for you and the other panelists to have one to two minutes to wrap up or get in the last word.

HANDOUTS

If you want your speech to be available as a handout, have it typed double-spaced with paragraph indentations, on 8½ × 11 paper, with each page numbered and the pages stapled. Identify your speech on the first page with your name, your title, the name of the group you're speaking to, the city, and the date of the speech. End each line of text with a complete word (no hyphens), thought or statistic, and end each page with a period. Write out abbreviations with hyphens (e.g., M-B-A or O-W-L [Older Women's League]) and if necessary, write out the words represented by the initials.

If the audience doesn't need your handout during your presentation, distribute it after you're finished. Otherwise, you'll be talking to the tops of heads as the audience reads your handout while you're talking.

If you use visuals, such as slides and overheads, you can make paper copies of them available as handouts. Sometimes such handouts are distributed before the presentation so that people in the audience can make notes on them.

A nice parting touch is to stand at the door as participants leave to give them your handout. Look them in the eye, shake their hands, and smile, and say you're glad they were there. It leaves a great last impression.

CONCLUSION

THE INGREDIENTS OF A GREAT PRESENTATION

1. Clear objective
2. Great open
3. Easy-to-follow body
4. Plenty of examples and/or stories
5. Memorable close
6. Transitions
7. Twenty-word-or-fewer sentences
8. Appropriate dress
9. Eye contact 90 to 100 percent of the time
10. Open face
11. Passion for your subject
12. A question-and-answer segment

Get turned on by your subject (see Figure 27). Be passionate about your subject, and let your passion and interest show. You want it to seem as if there is nowhere else in the world you'd rather be than with your audience, sharing your information and expertise.

Study other presenters and public speakers, including spell-binding clergy, to learn from them. Notice how they tell stories, emphasize key points, vary their voices, gesture, and pace themselves.

Smile, if appropriate, or have an open facial expression, gesture, and make eye contact as much as possible. Be emotional, excited, enthusiastic, entertaining, and eager. If you aren't, the audience won't do, think, or feel whatever it is that you want it to.

Figure 27.   Get turned on to your subject.

Being a good speaker is learnable. You can speak with pride, conviction, and persuasiveness. You can be a charismatic, commanding, compelling, credible, enthusiastic, outstanding, passionate, and powerful speaker. *But*—you must know your topic and be very clear about your objective. You must know to whom you're talking. And you must practice. Think of a public appearance as a glorious golden opportunity, not a burden.

If you follow this advice, you will feel successful and triumphant at the end of your next presentation as the audience applauds and says, "Bravo!"

The 10 Steps to a Great Presentation

1. Determine the purpose or objective of your presentation—what you want the audience to know. Write it down in a sentence of twenty-five words or fewer.